ARTIST TRANSCRIPTIONS GUITAR

BEST OF Herb Ellis

Cover photo © Burt Goldblatt Estate Archives/CTSIMAGES

Music transcriptions by
Pete Billmann, Jeff Jacobson, Ron Piccione and David Stocker

ISBN 978-1-4803-8364-7

HAL•LEONARD® CORPORATION

7777 W. BLUEMOUND RD. P.O. BOX 13819 MILWAUKEE, WI 53213

Visit Hal Leonard Online at
www.halleonard.com

CONTENTS

from *Straight Ahead*

Captain Bill

By Herb Ellis, Monty Alexander and Ray Brown

*Chord symbols reflect implied harmony.

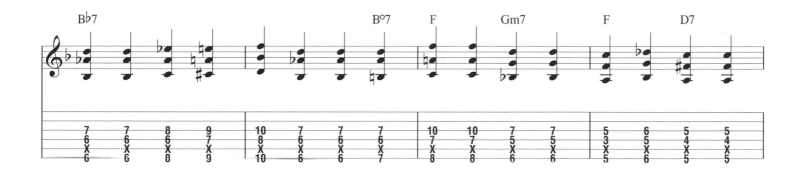

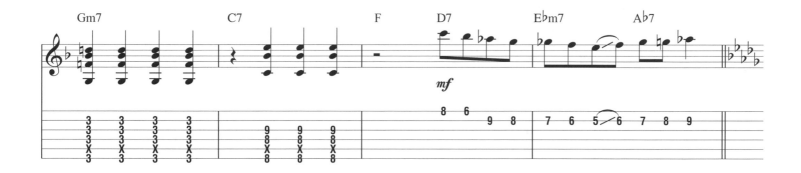

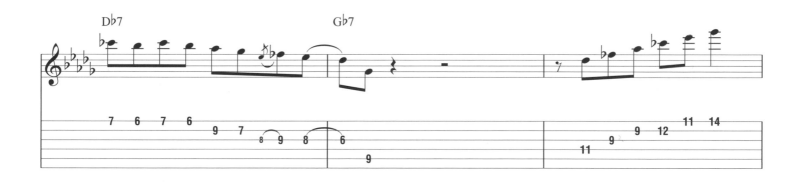

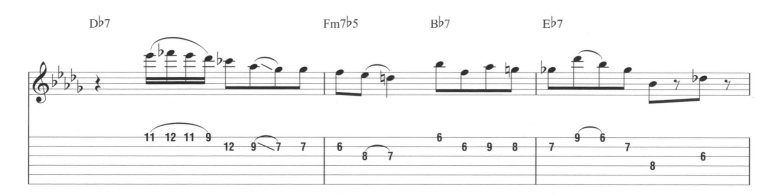

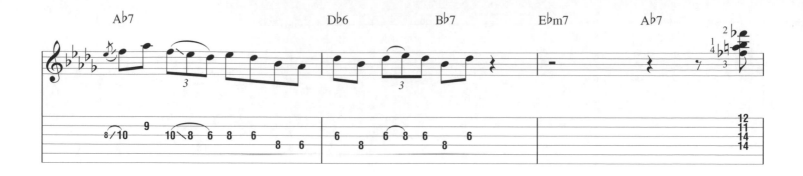

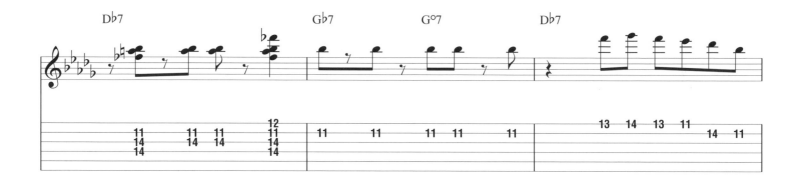

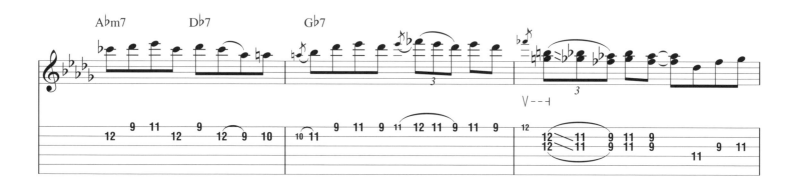

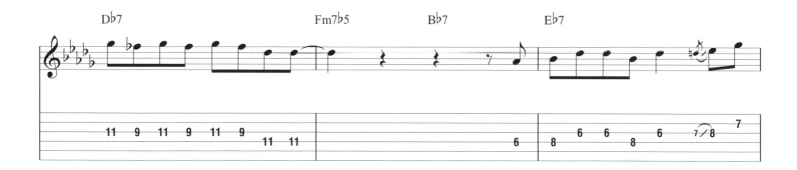

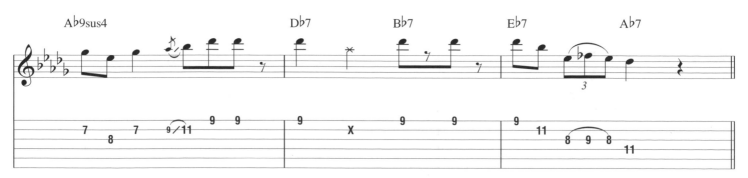

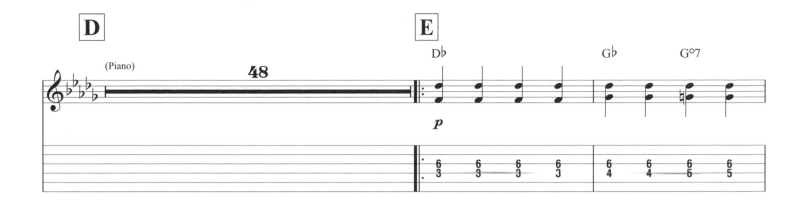

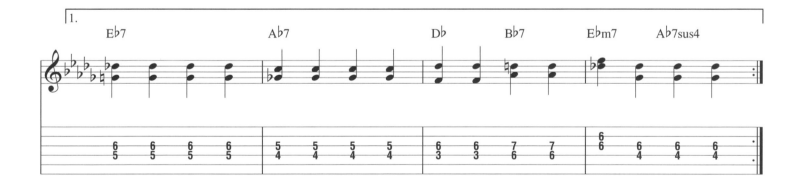

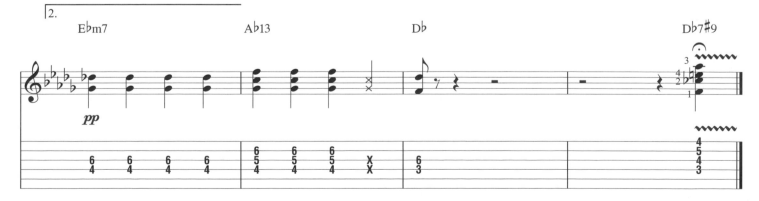

from *Herb Mix*
Deep
By Herb Ellis

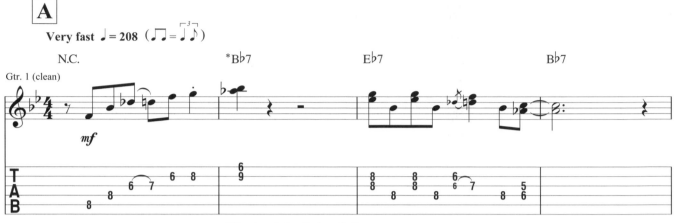

*Chord symbols reflect implied harmony.

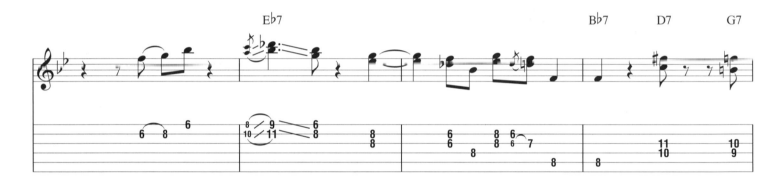

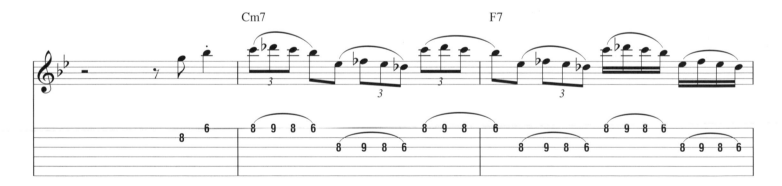

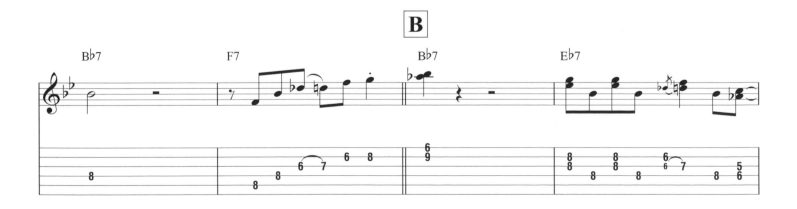

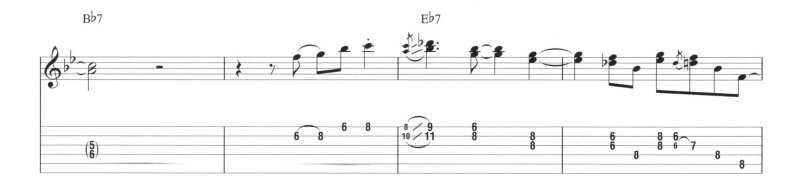

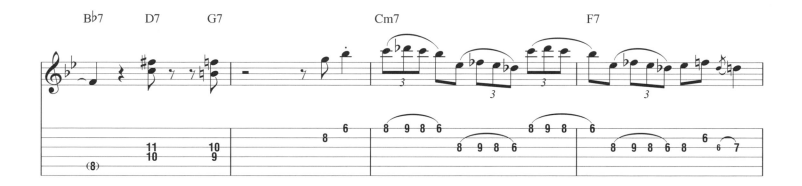

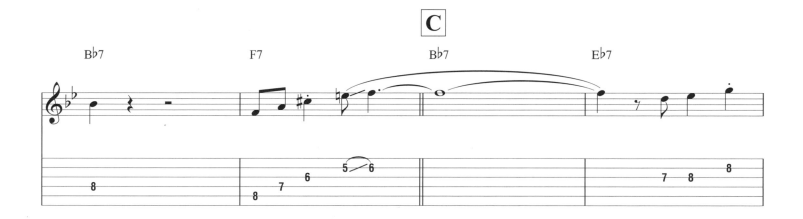

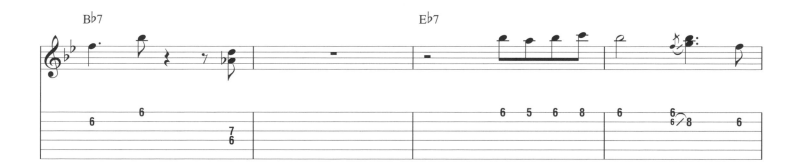

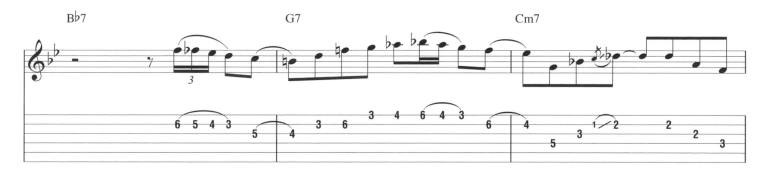

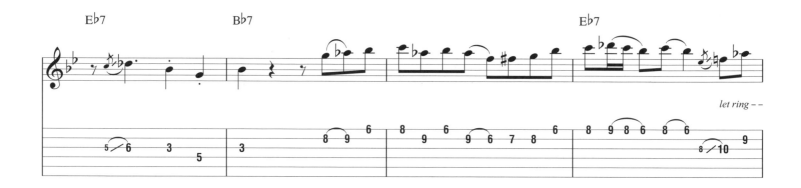

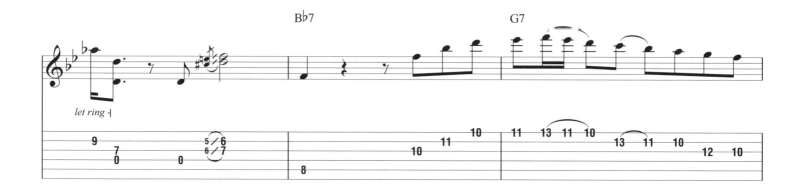

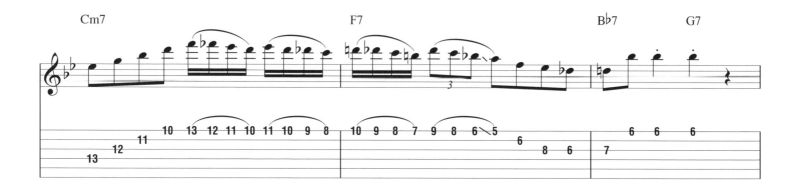

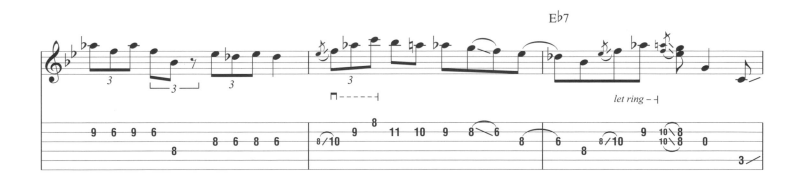

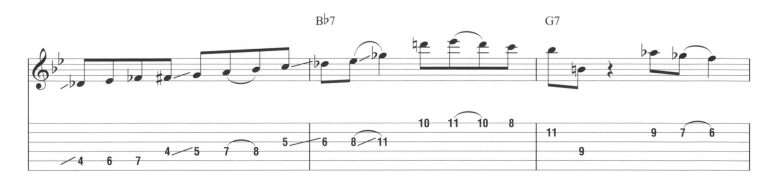

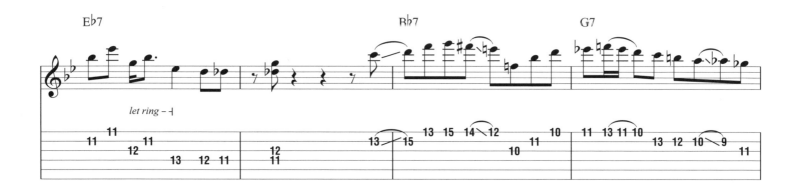

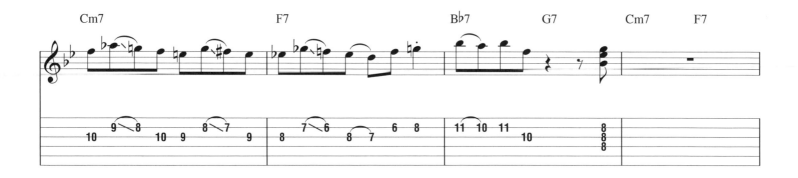

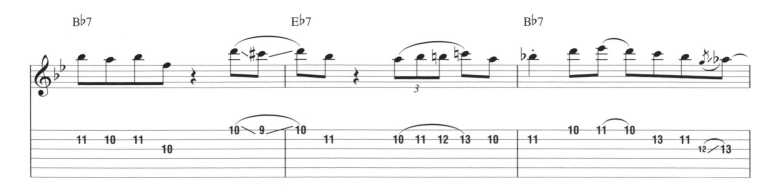

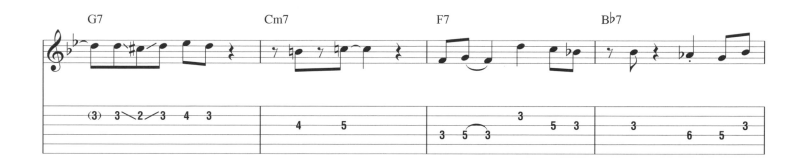

D

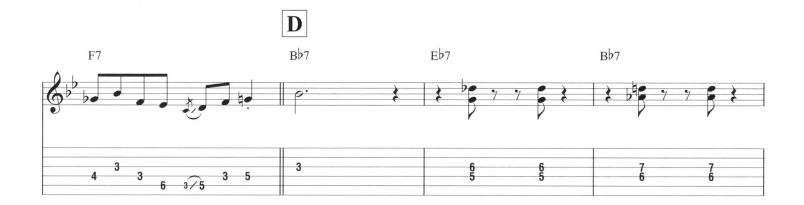

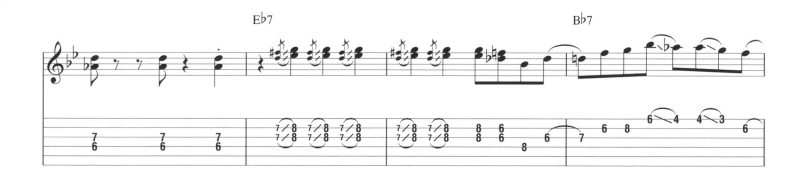

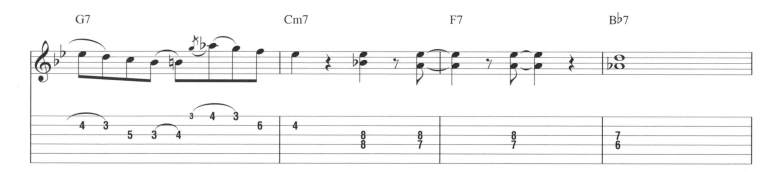

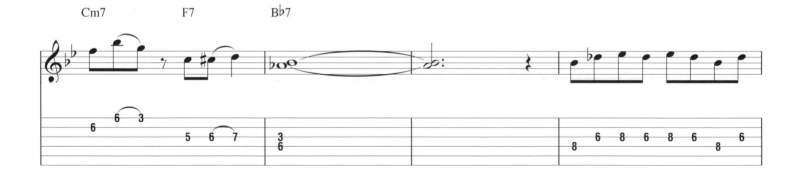

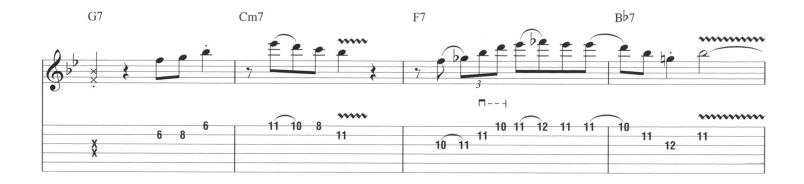

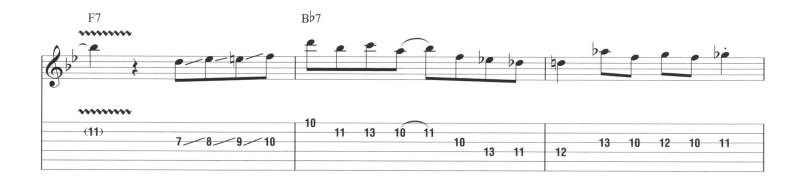

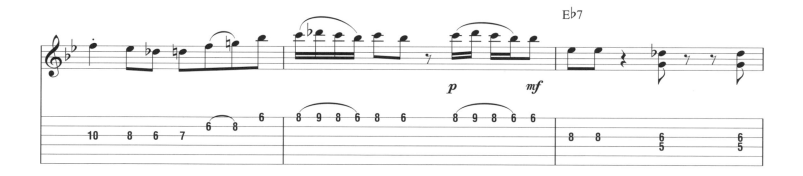

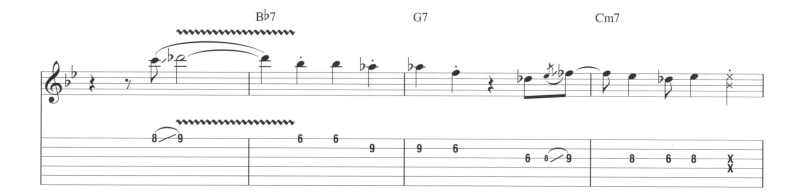

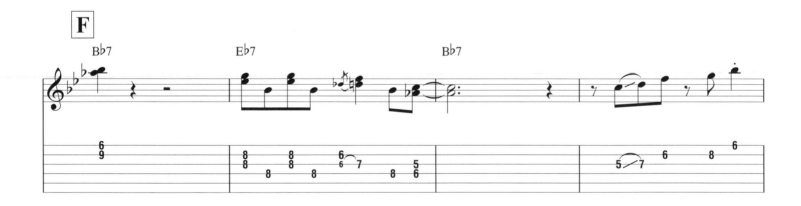

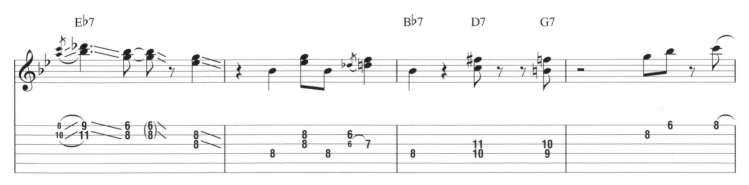

16

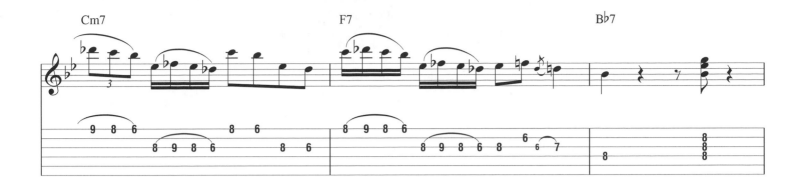

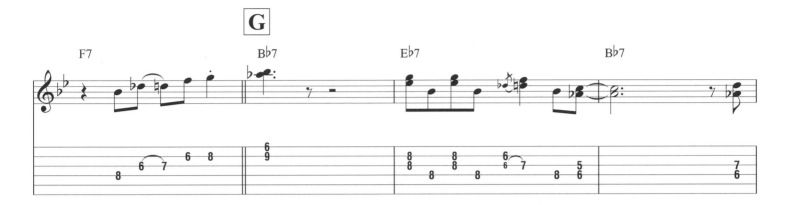

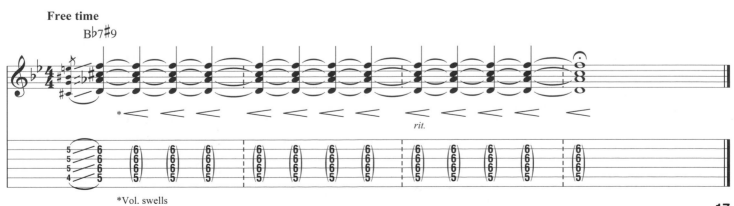

Detour Ahead

from *Ellis in Wonderland*

By Herb Ellis, John Frigo and Lou Carter

*Chord symbols reflect overall harmony.

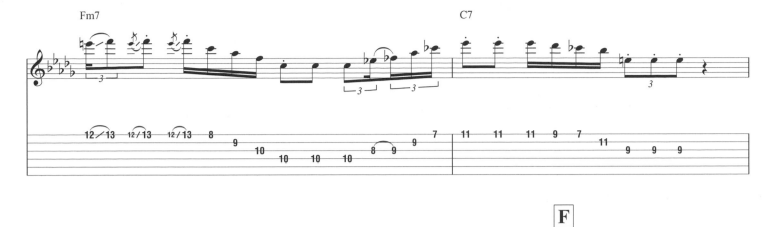

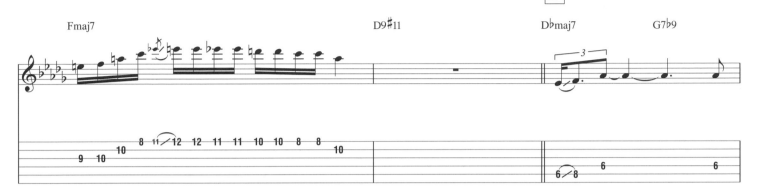

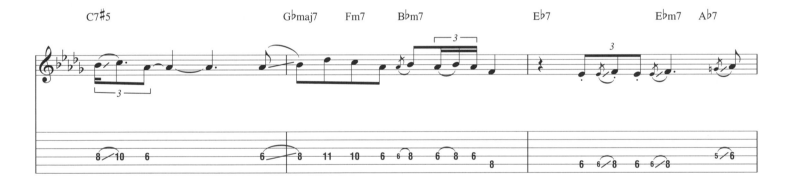

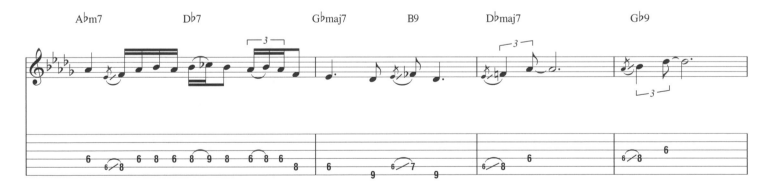

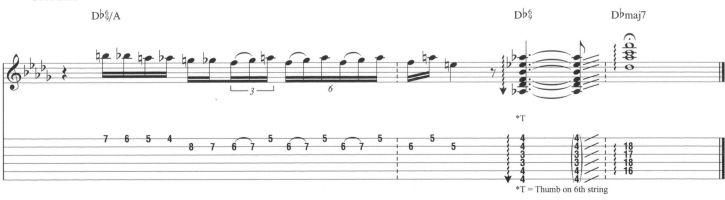

*T = Thumb on 6th string

from *Soft Shoe*
Easter Parade
Words and Music by Irving Berlin

* Tempo fluctuates between 62-84 b.p.m.

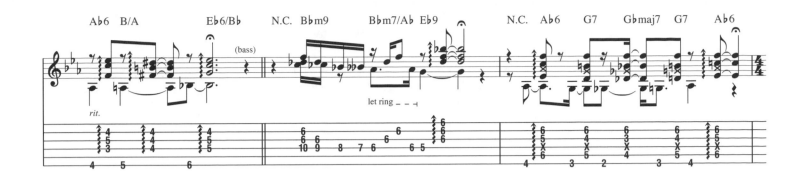

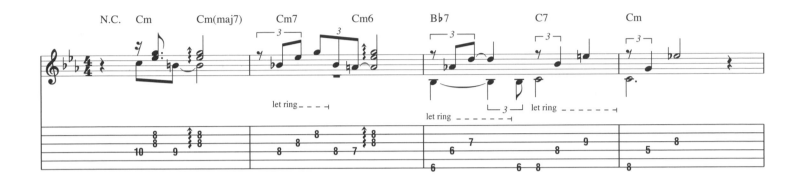

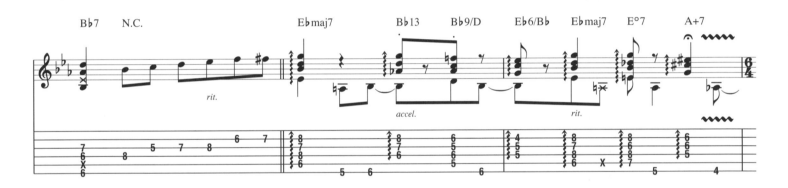

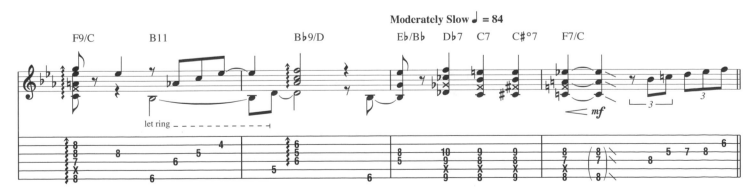

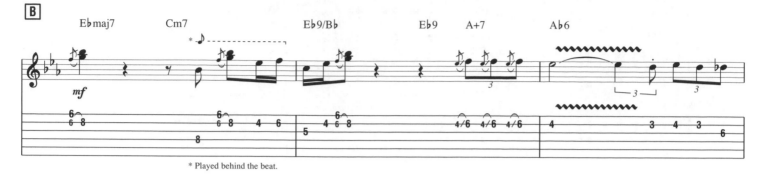

* Played behind the beat.

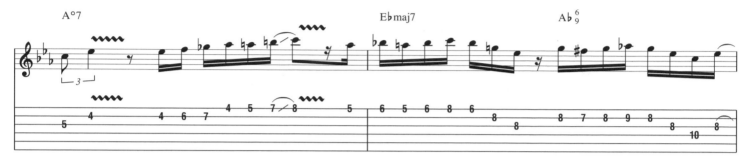

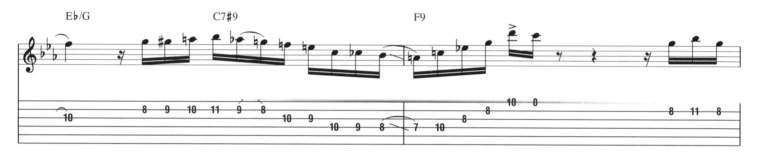

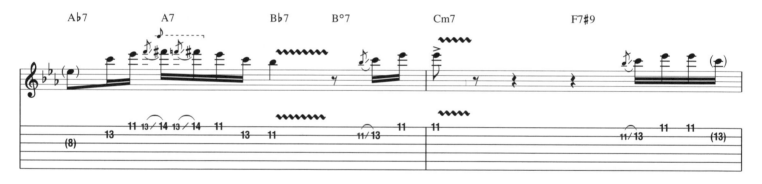

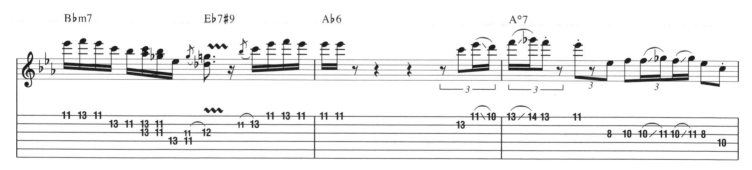

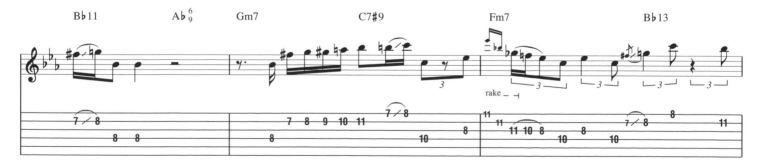

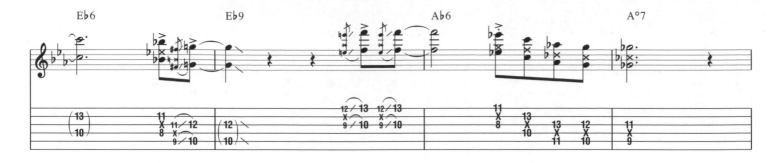

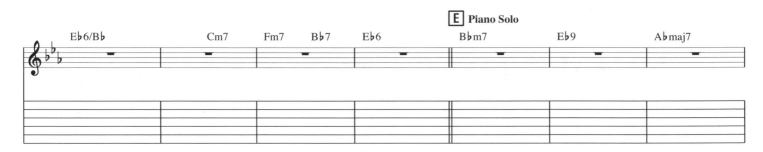

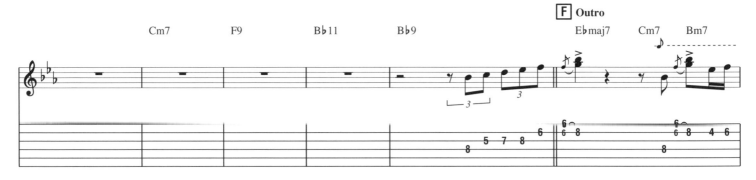

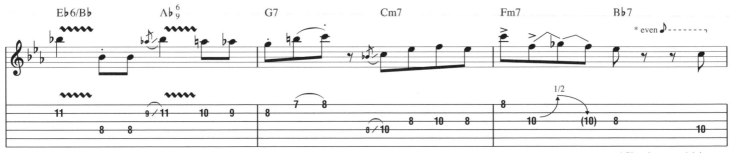

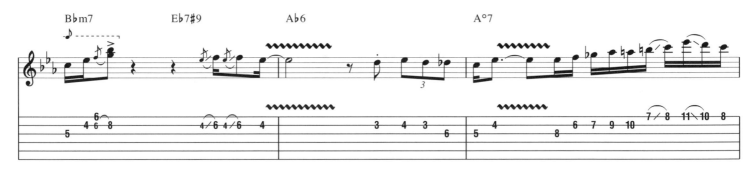

* Played as even eighth notes.

Ellis in Wonderland

By Herb Ellis

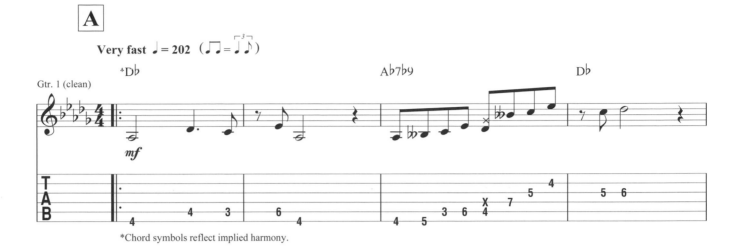

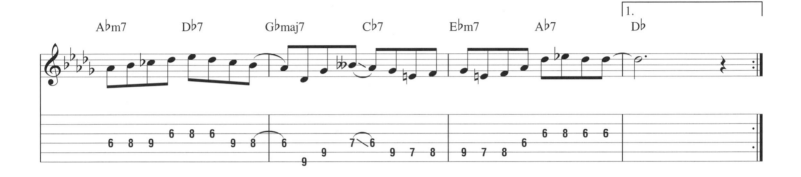

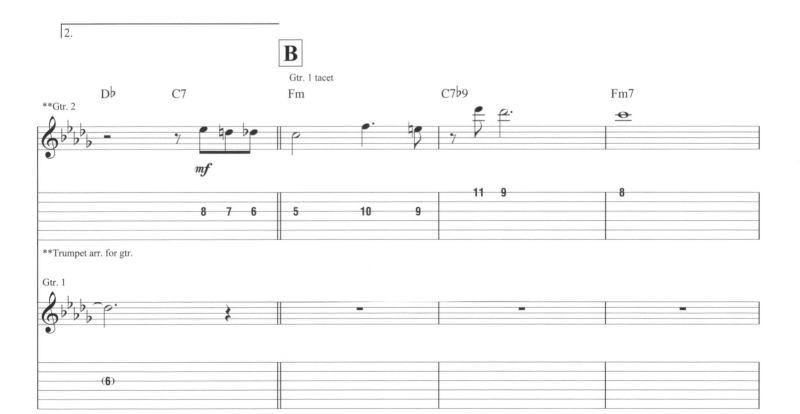

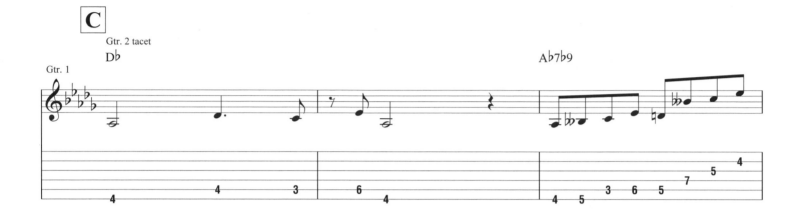

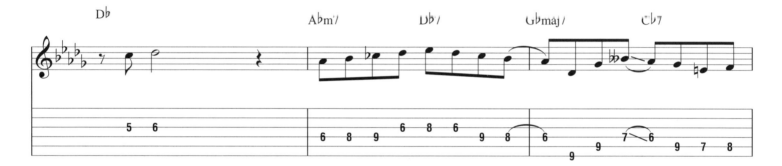

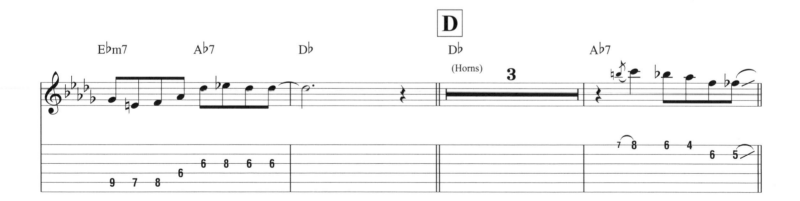

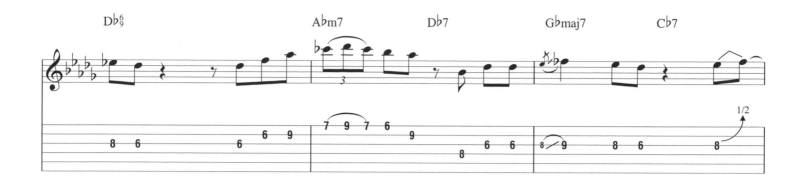

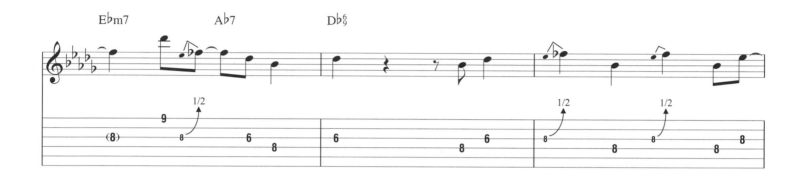

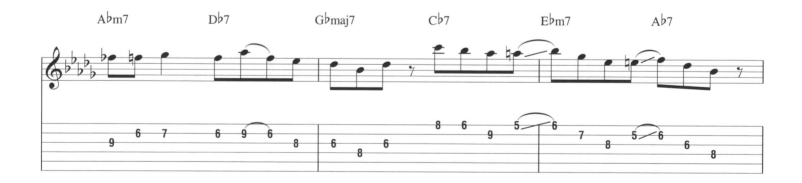

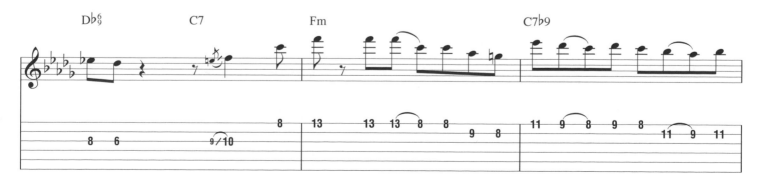

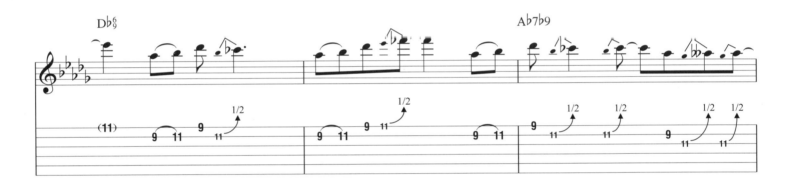

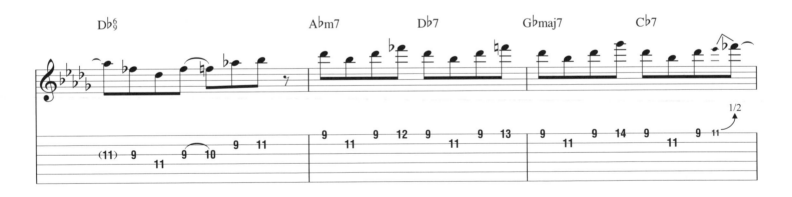

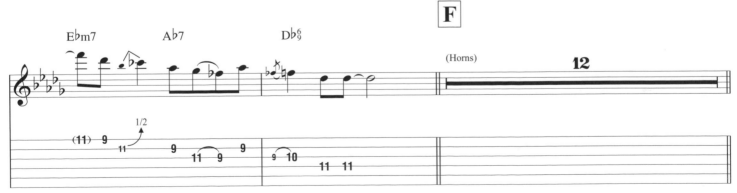

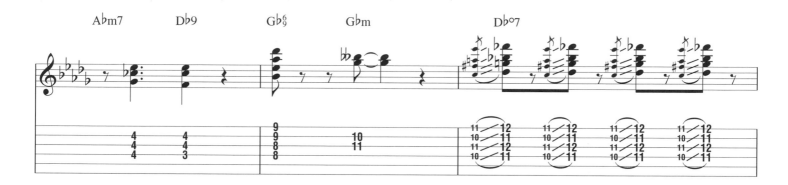

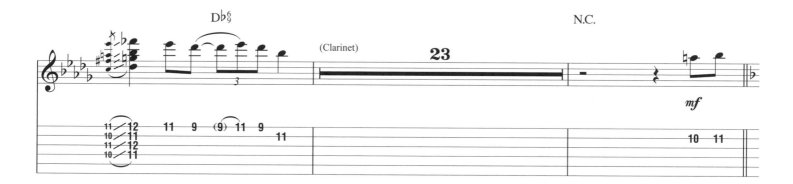

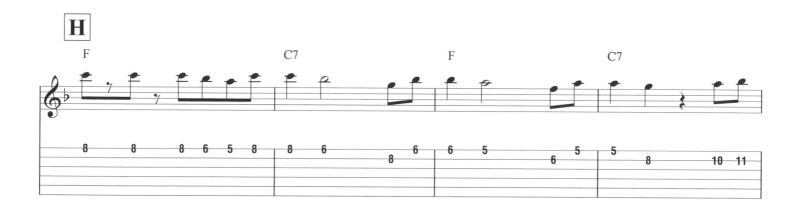

I

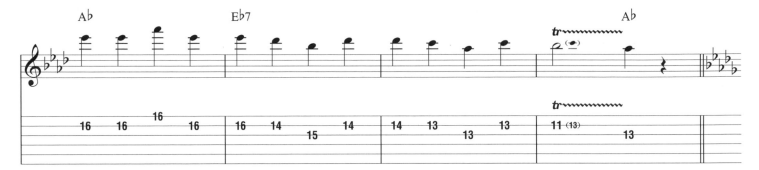

J

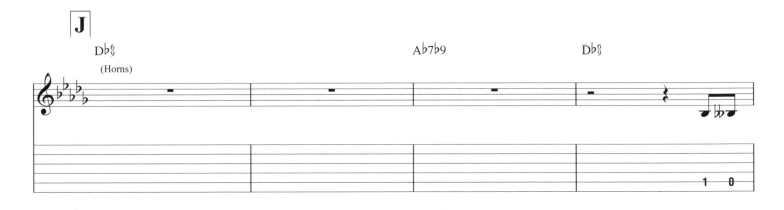

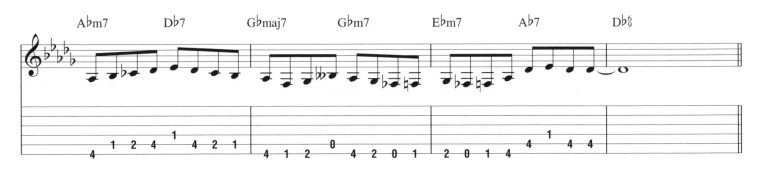

K

Gtr. 1 tacet

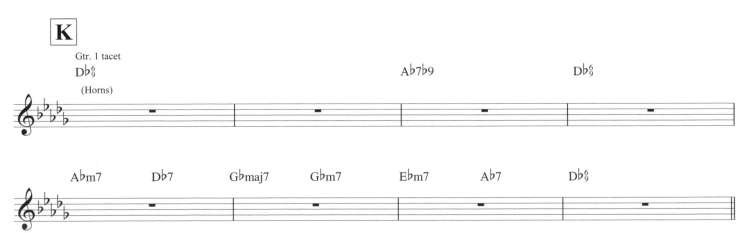

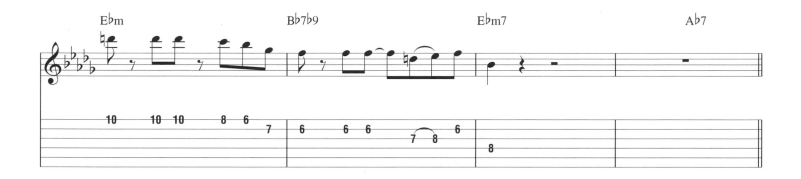

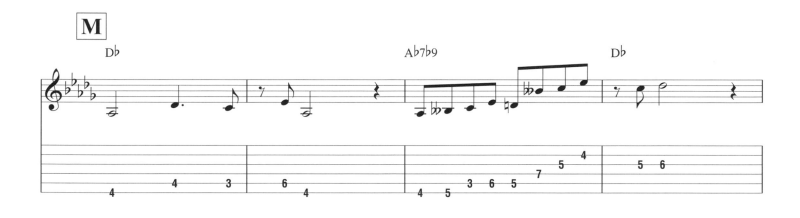

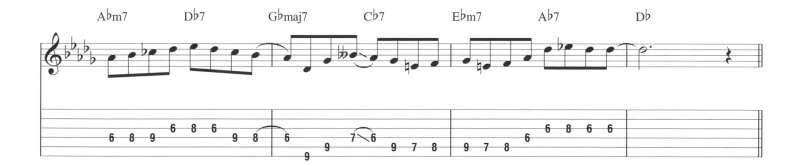

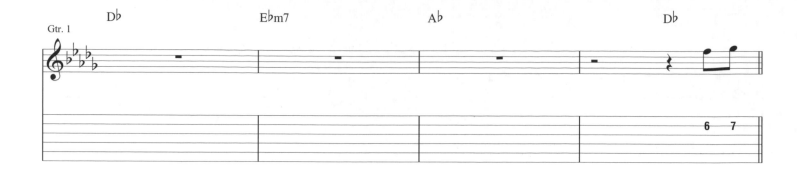

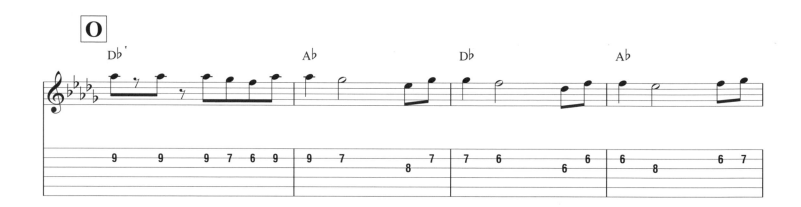

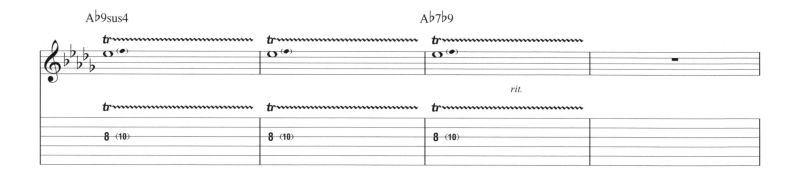

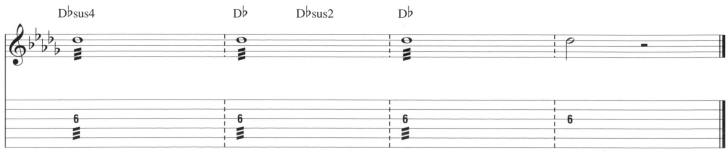

from *Ellis in Wonderland*

It Could Happen to You

from the Paramount Picture AND THE ANGELS SING

Words by Johnny Burke
Music by James Van Heusen

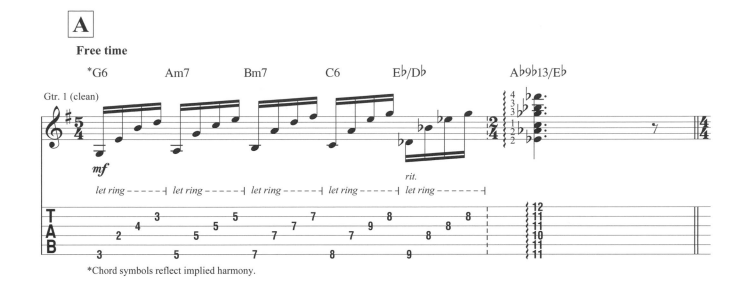

*Chord symbols reflect implied harmony.

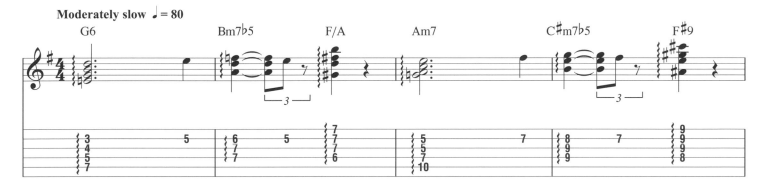

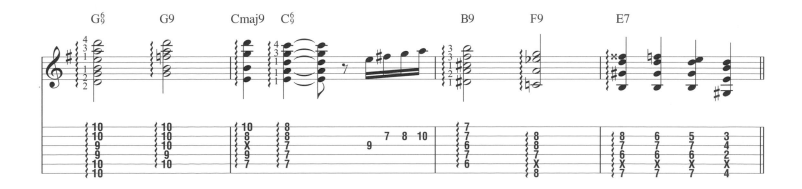

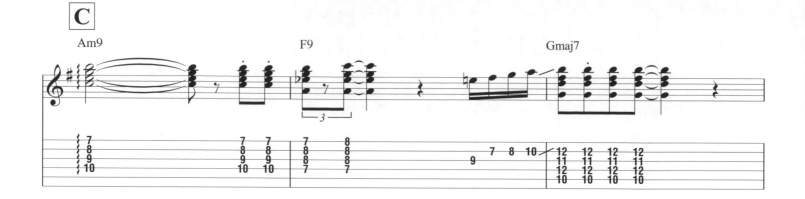

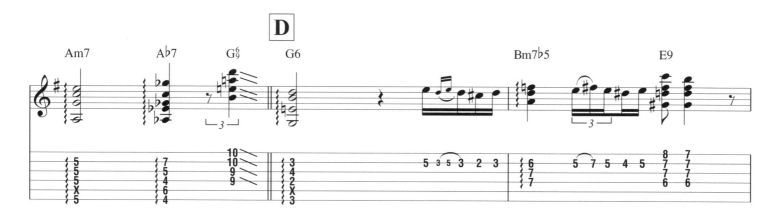

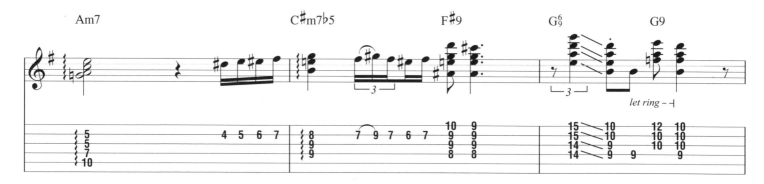

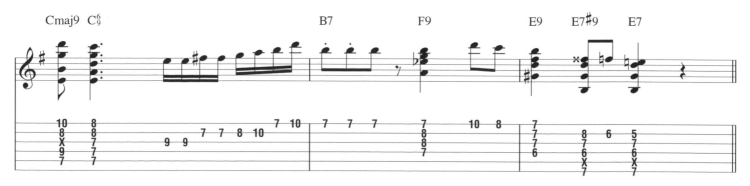

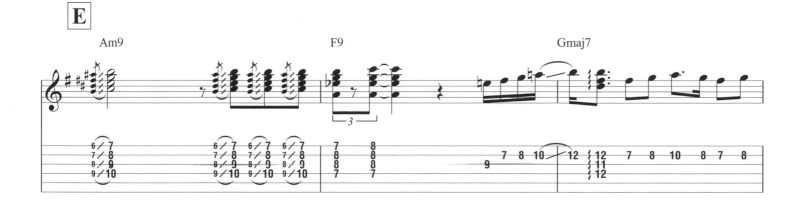

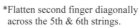

*Flatten second finger diagonally
across the 5th & 6th strings.

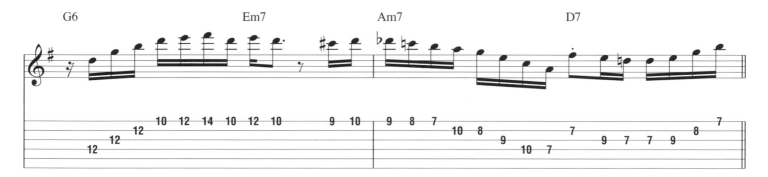

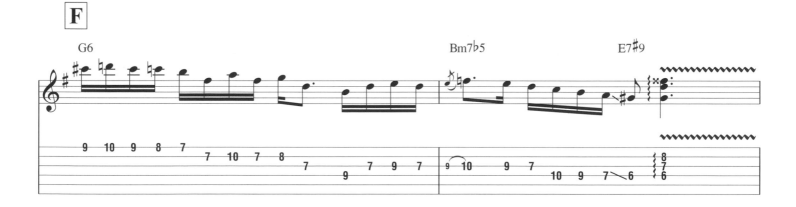

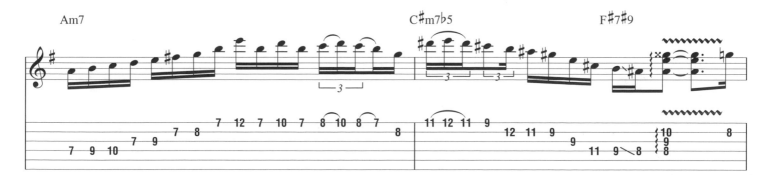

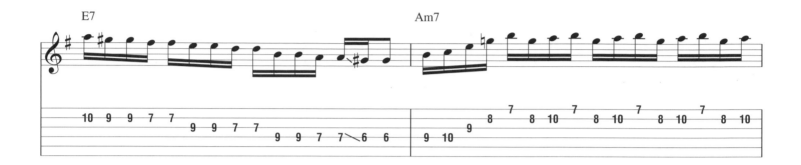

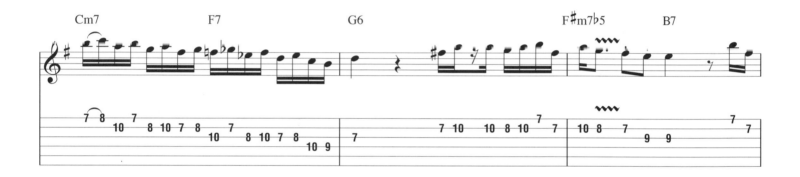

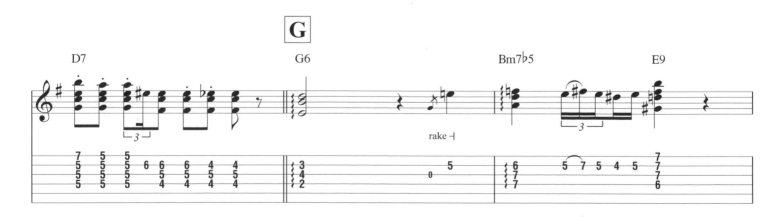

38

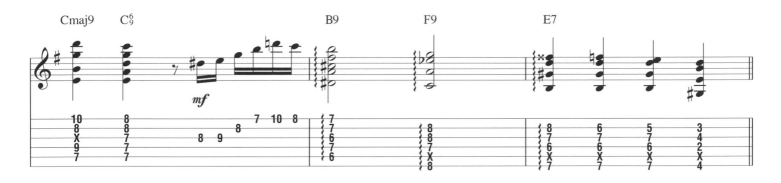

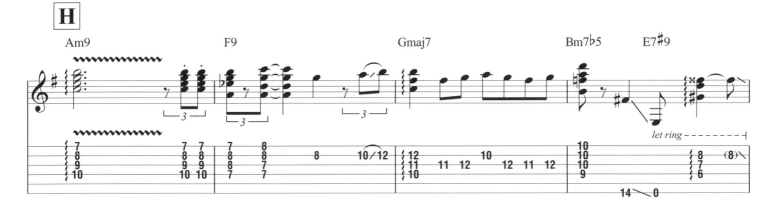

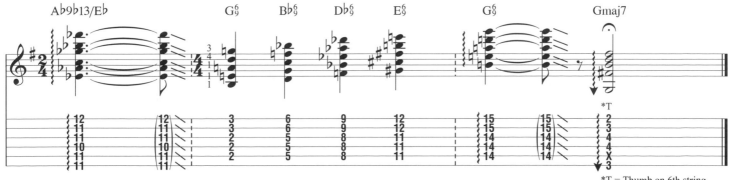

*T = Thumb on 6th string

from *Two for the Road*

Love for Sale

Words and Music by Cole Porter

*Joe Pass   **Chord symbols reflect implied harmony.

***Herb Ellis

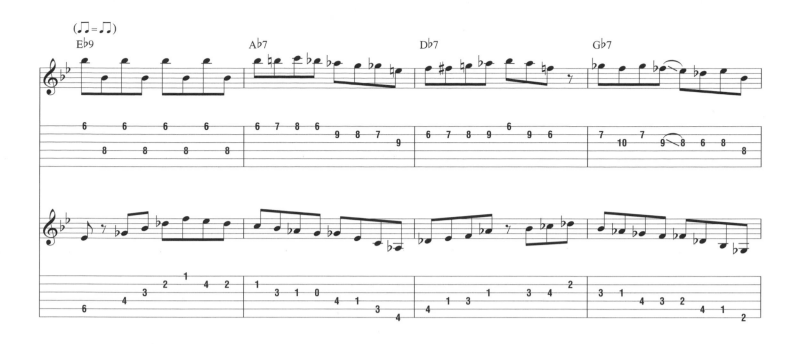

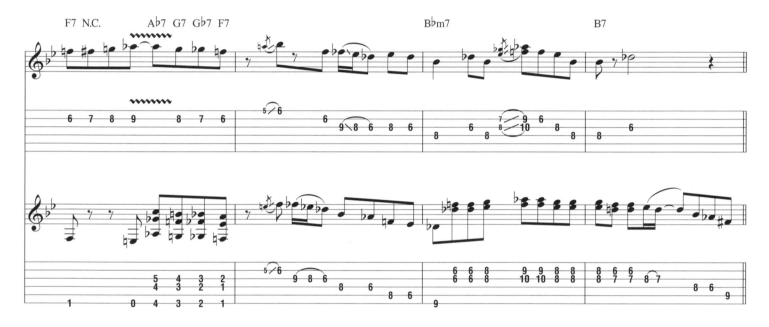

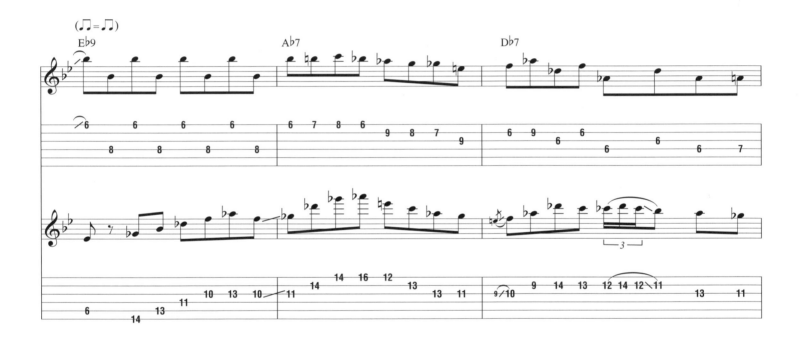

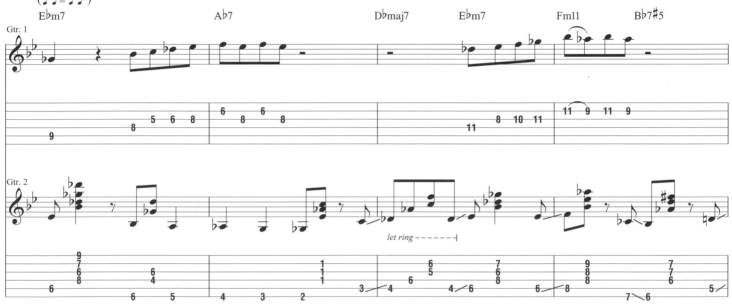

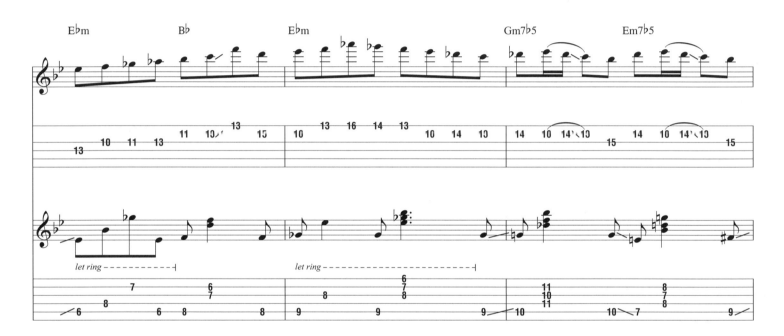

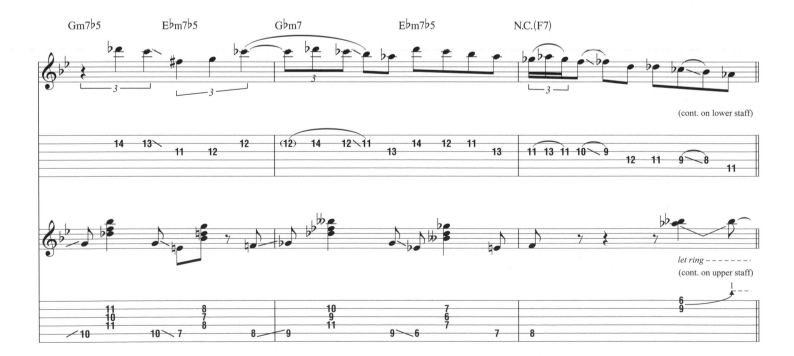

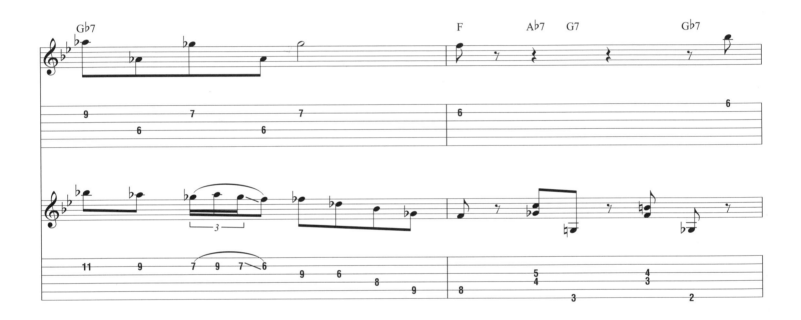

E

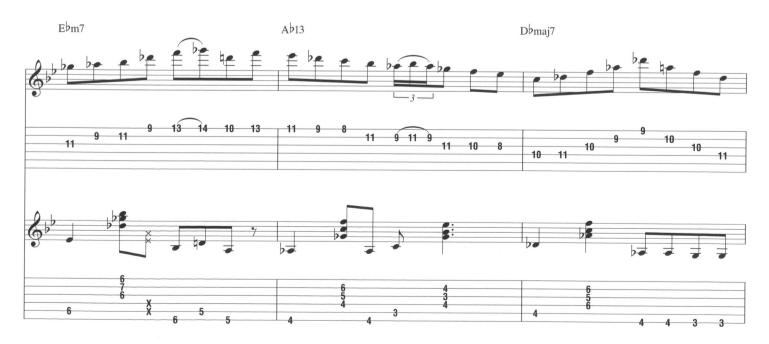

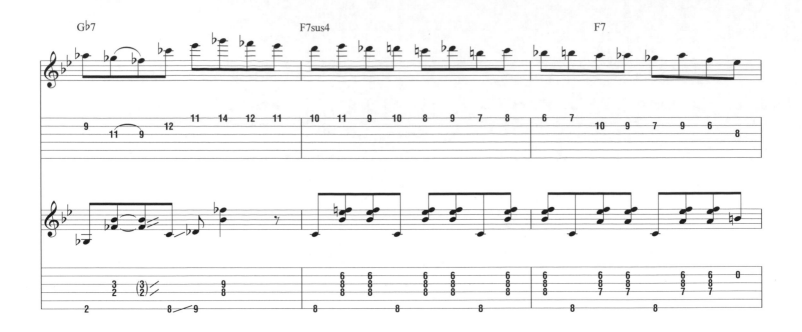

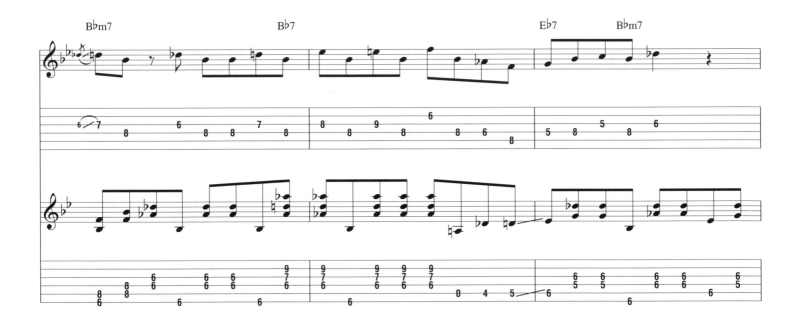

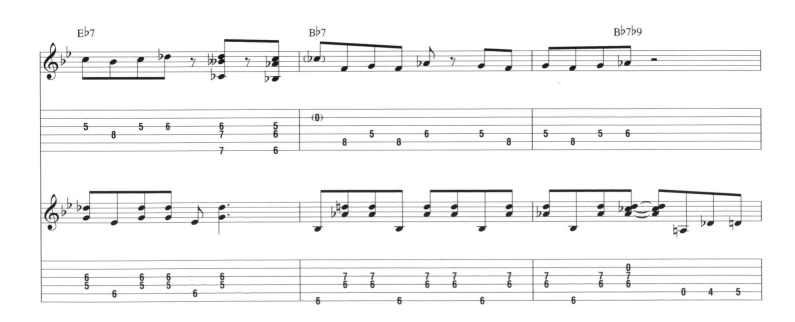

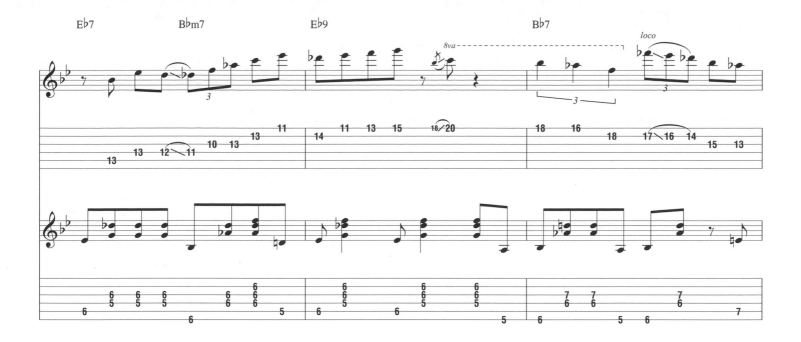

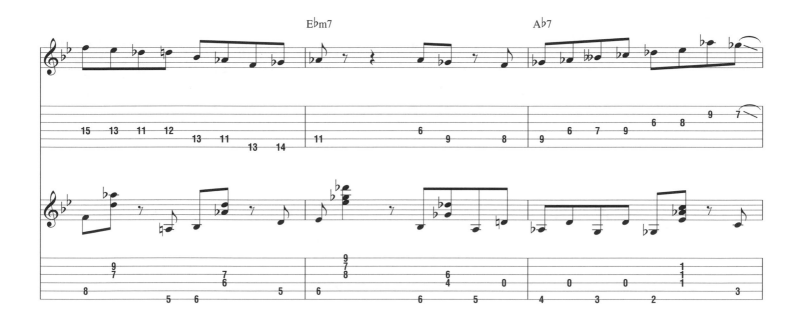

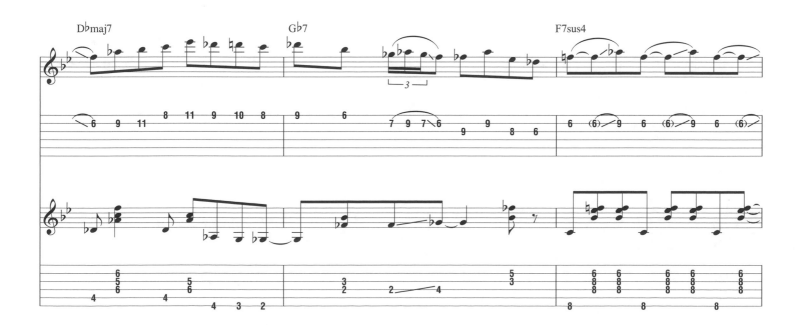

*Barre 1st & 2nd strings with fret-hand 4th finger.

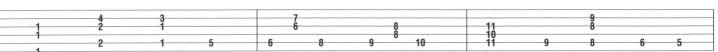

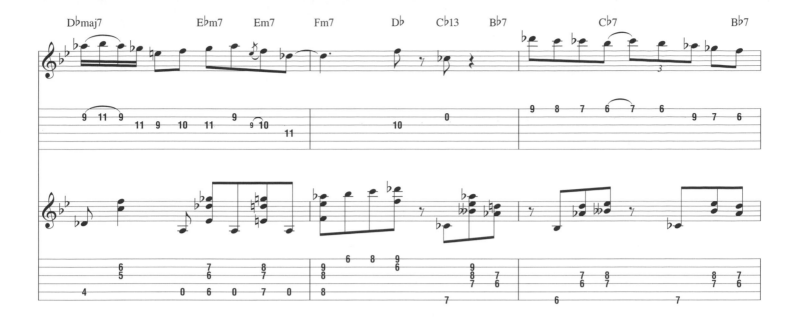

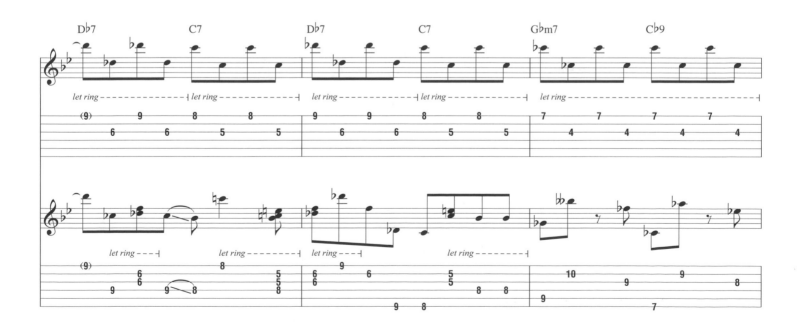

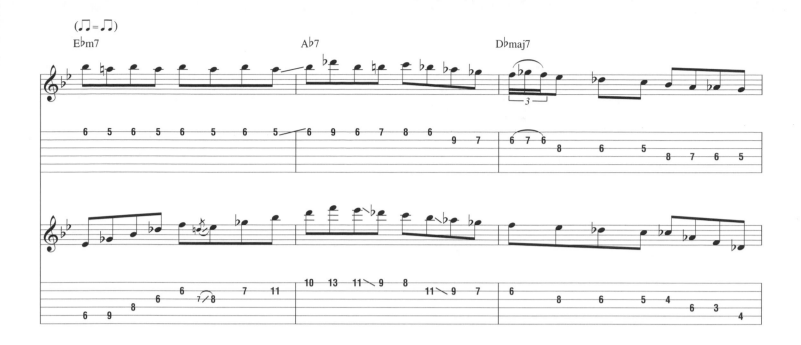

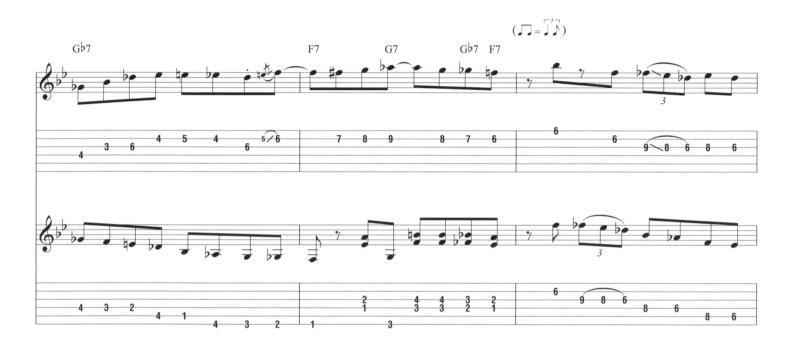

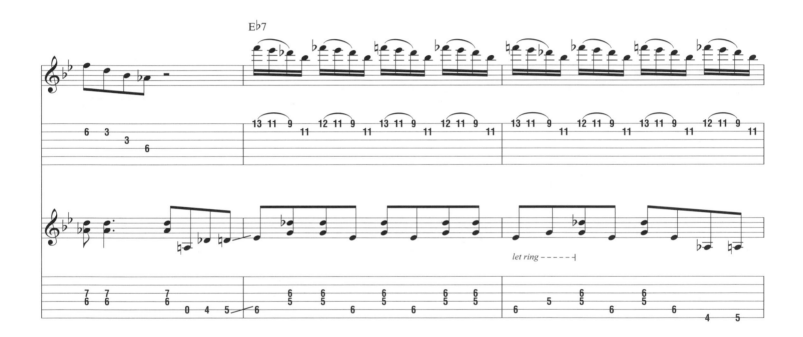

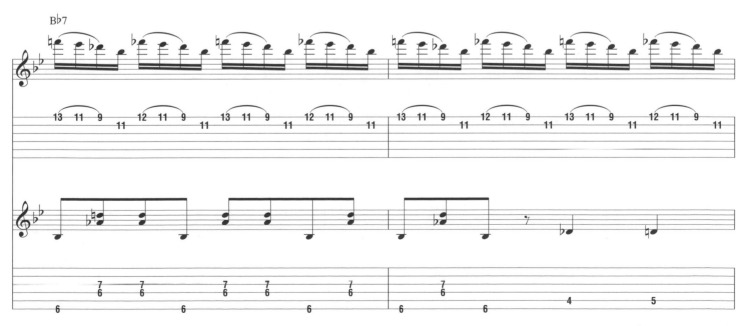

I

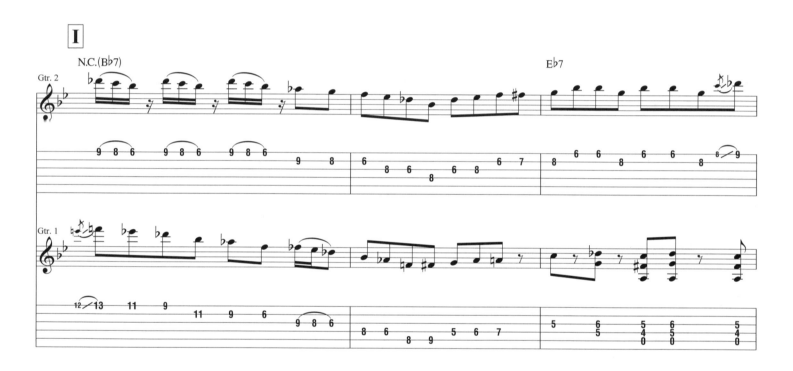

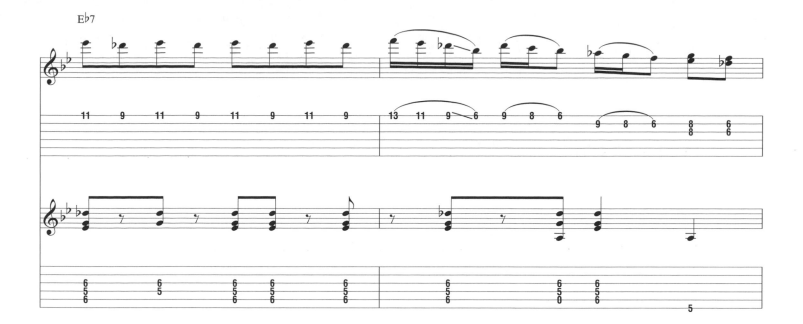

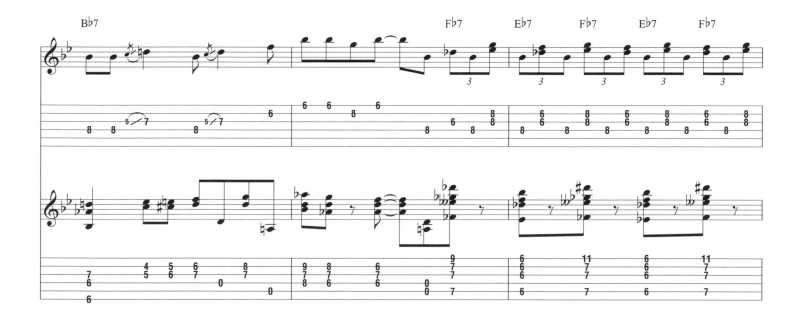

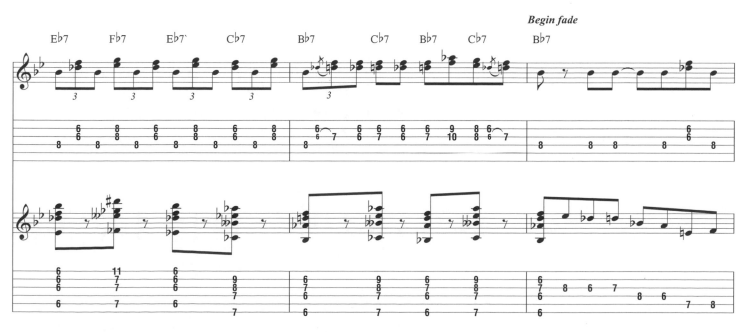

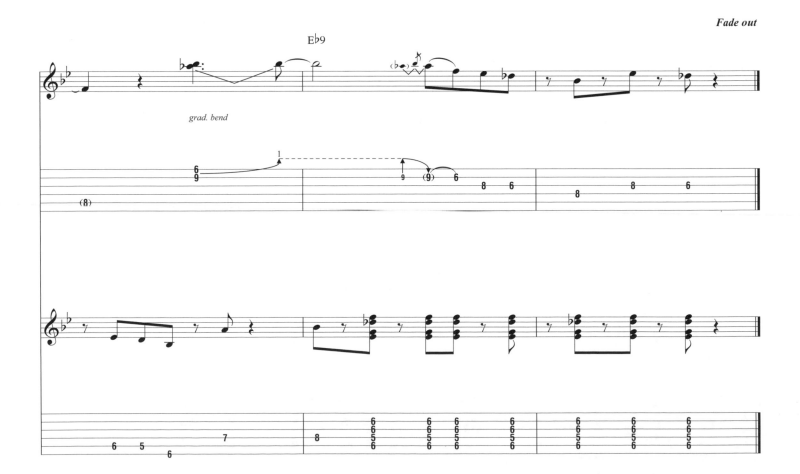

from *Hello Herbie (with Oscar Peterson)*

Naptown Blues

By John L. (Wes) Montgomery

*Chord symbols reflect implied harmony.

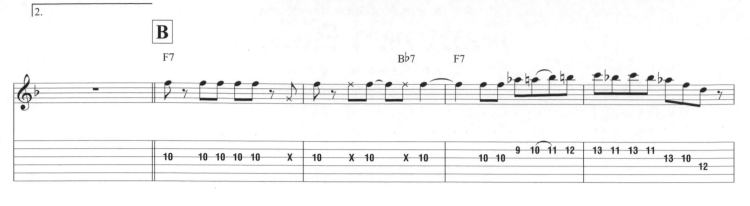

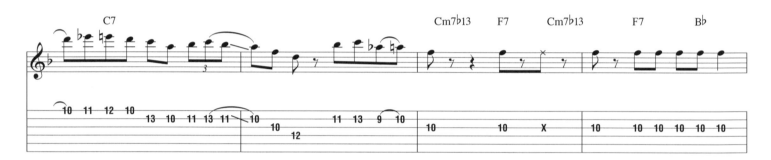

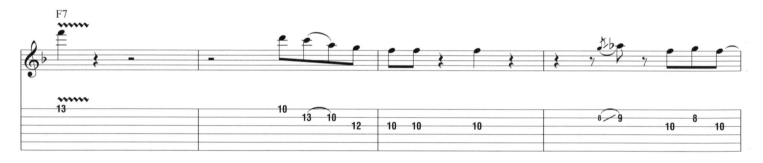

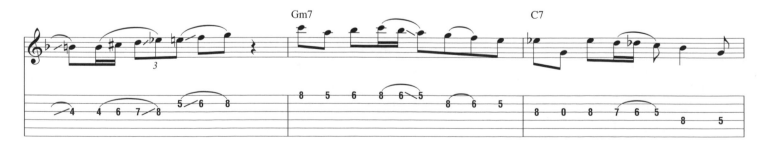

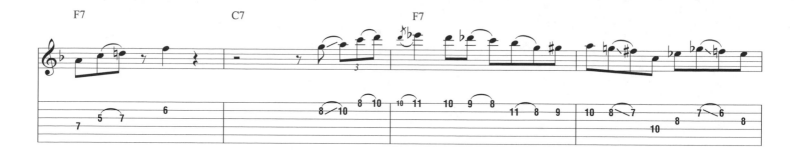

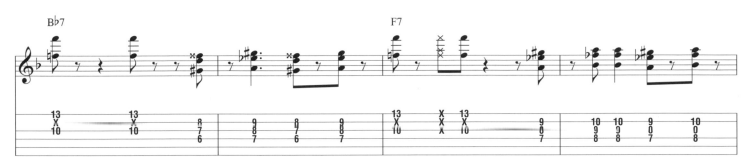

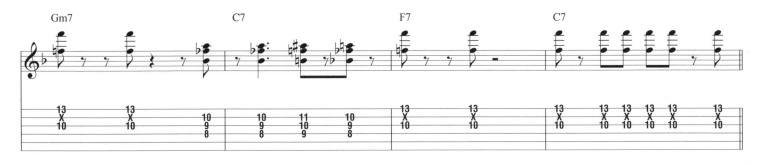

D

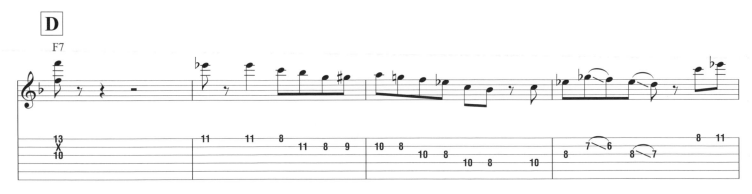

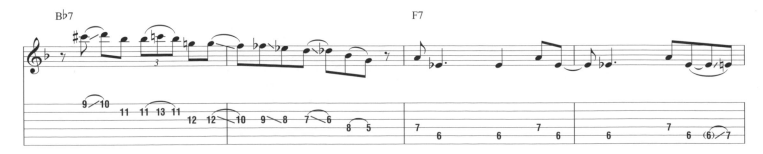

E

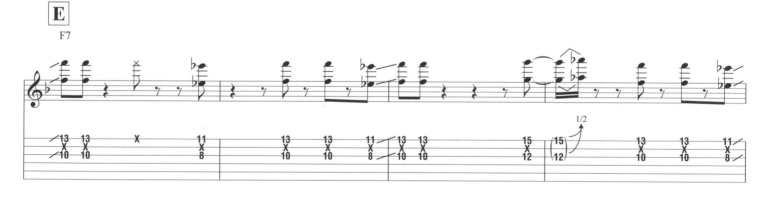

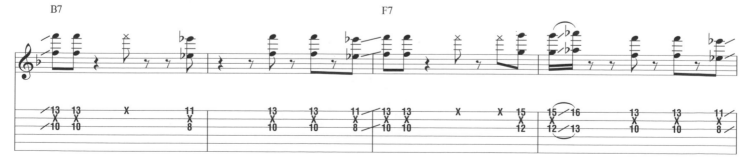

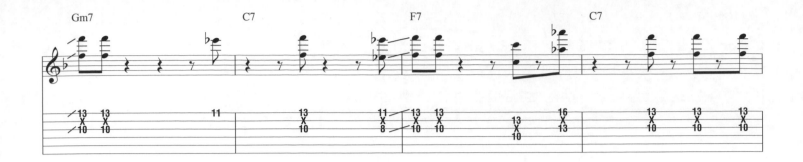

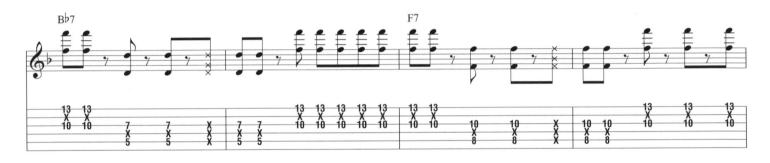

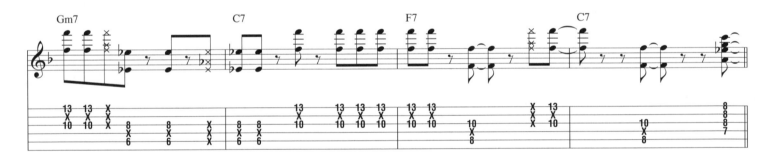

F

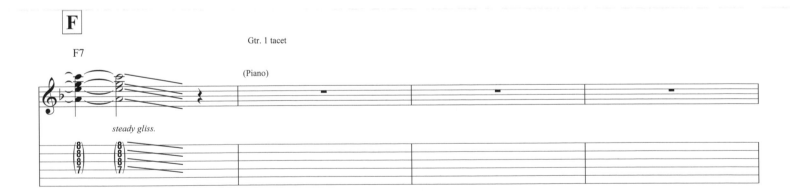

64

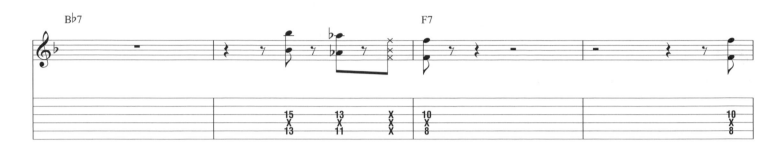

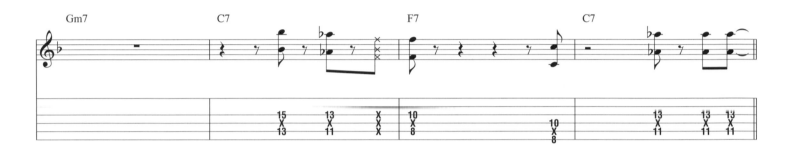

I

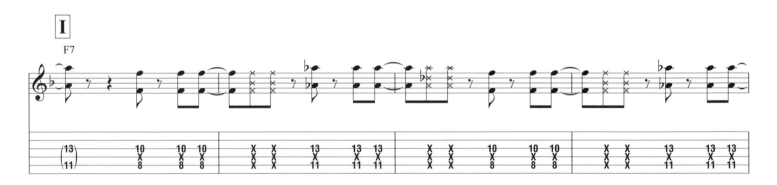

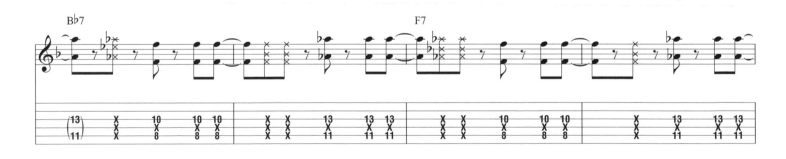

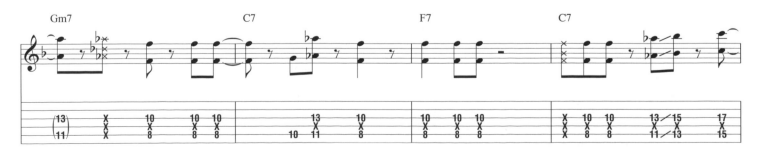

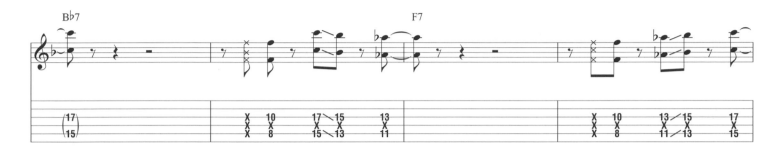

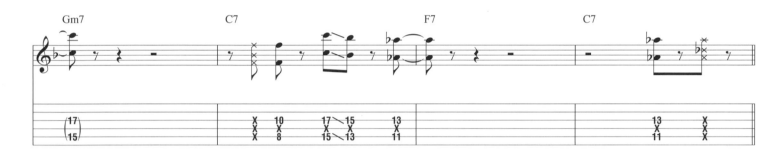

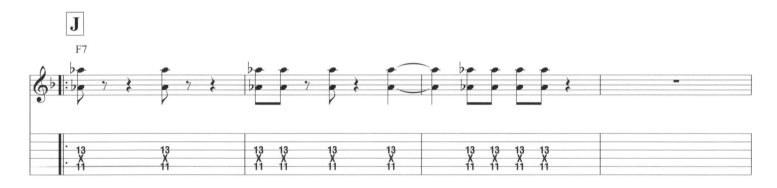

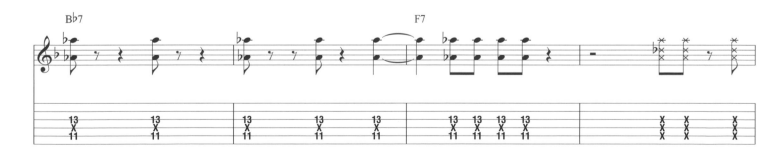

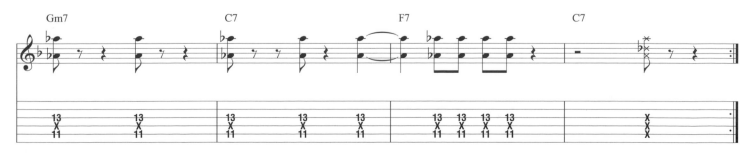

K

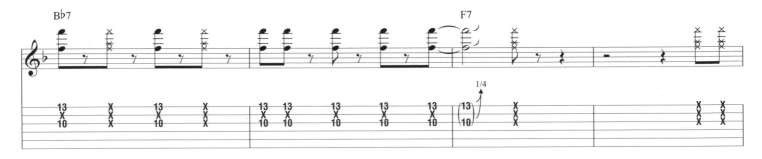

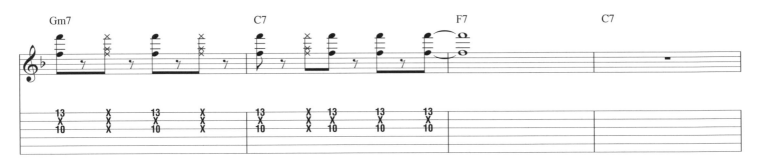

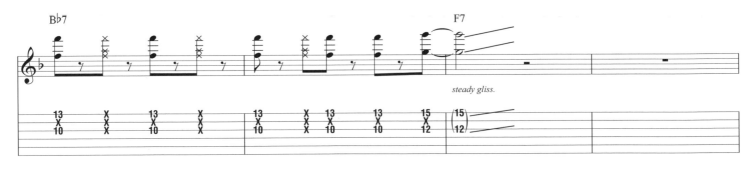

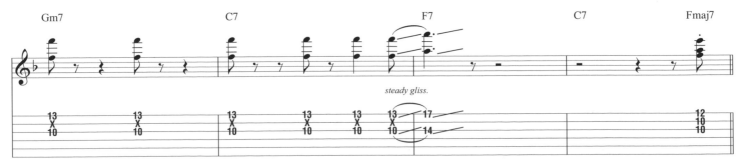

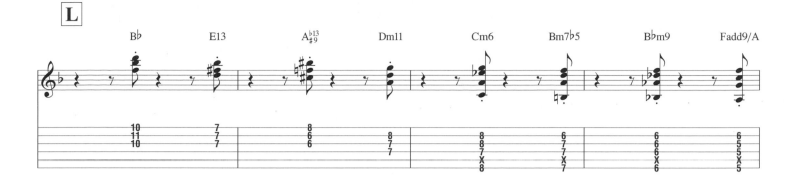

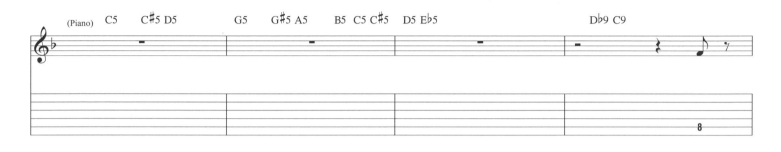

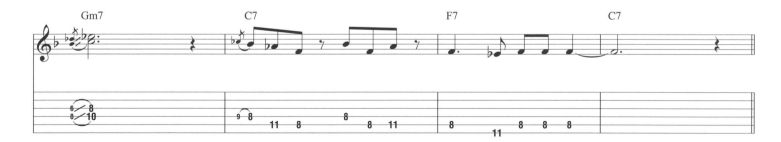

M

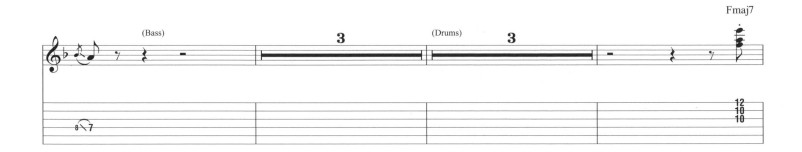

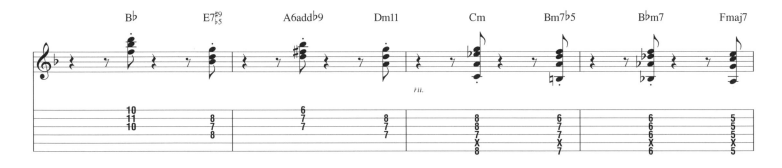

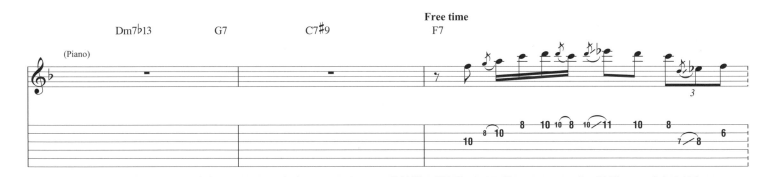

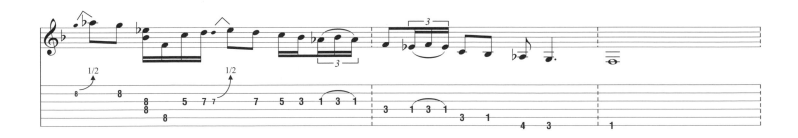

from *Softly...But with That Feeling*

One Note Samba

(Samba De Uma Nota So)

Original Lyrics by Newton Mendonça
English Lyrics by Antonio Carlos Jobim
Music by Antonio Carlos Jobim

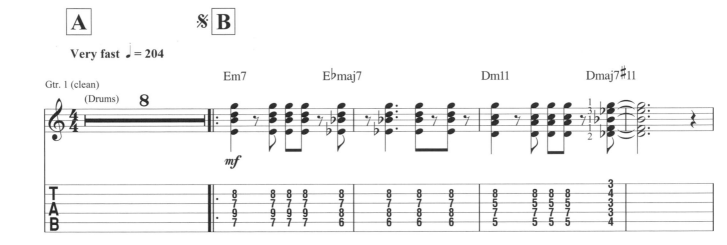

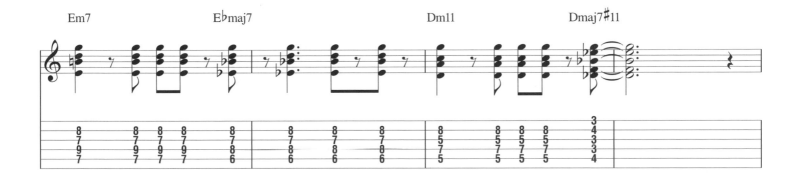

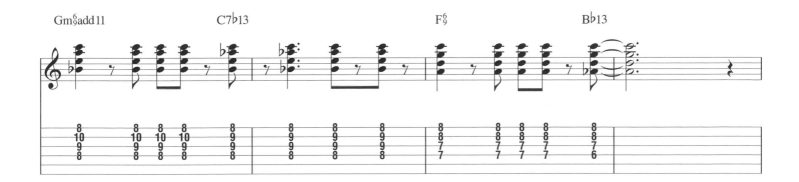

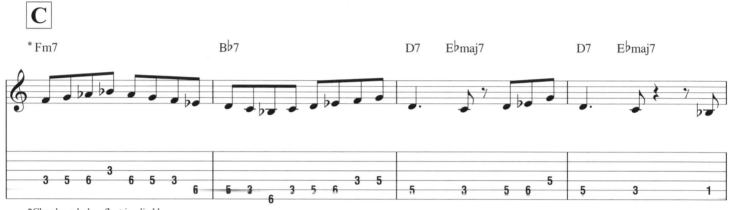

*Chord symbols reflect implied harmony.

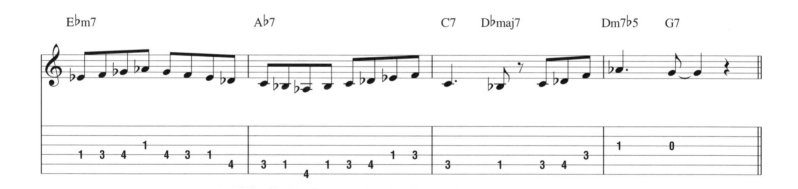

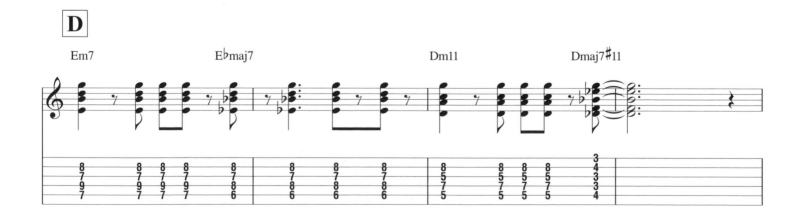

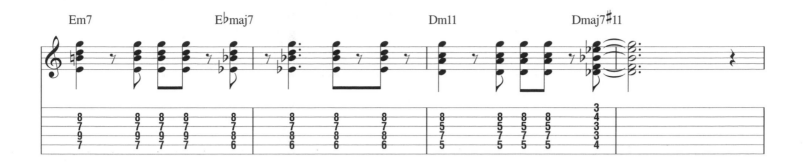

To Coda ⊕

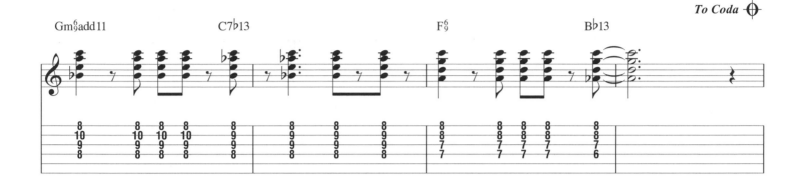

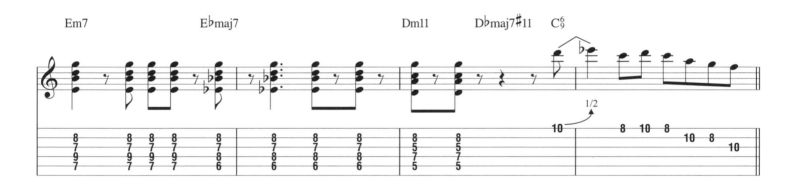

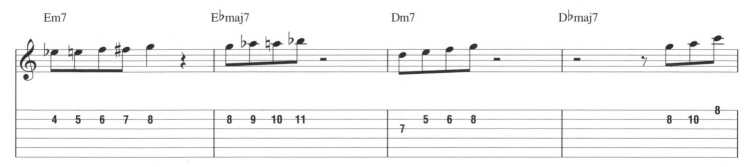

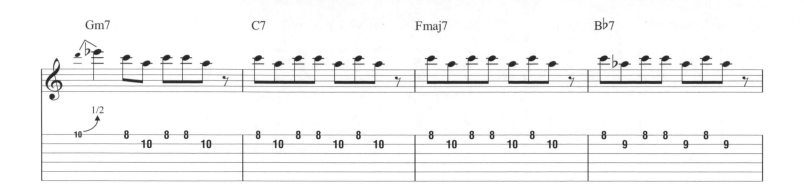

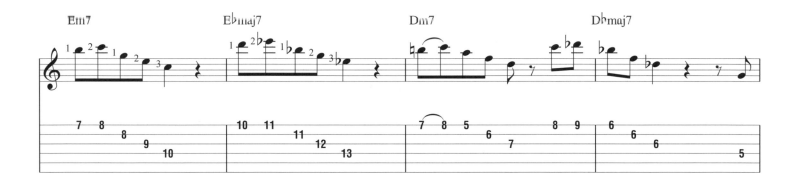

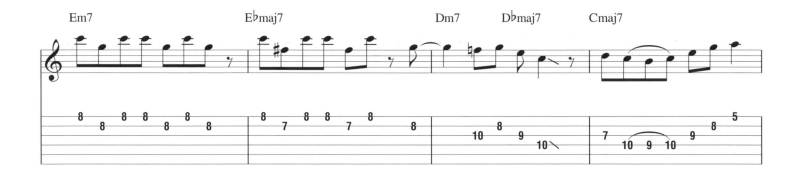

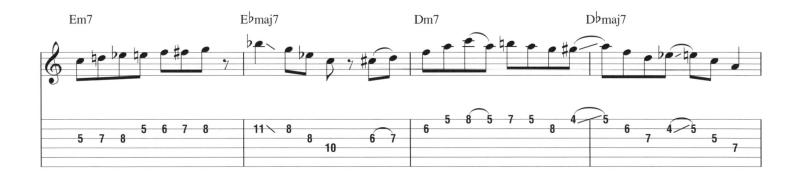

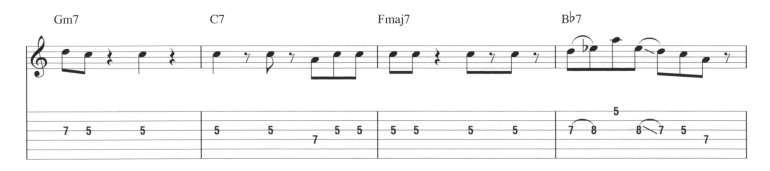

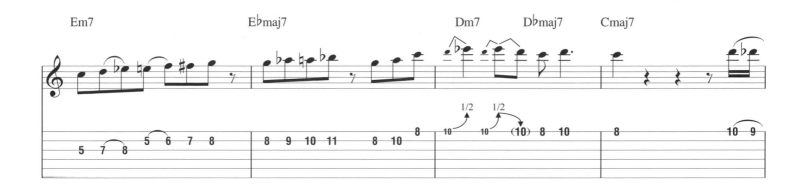

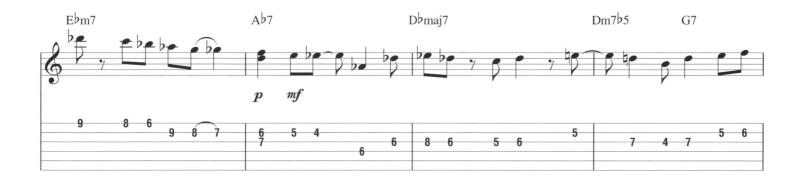

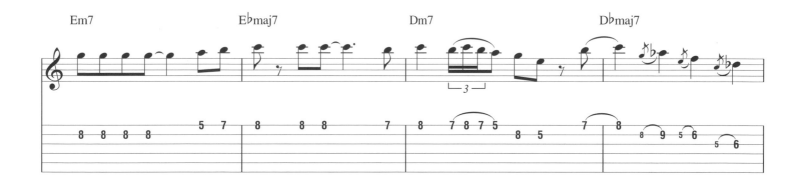

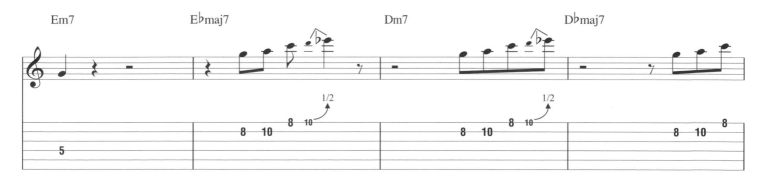

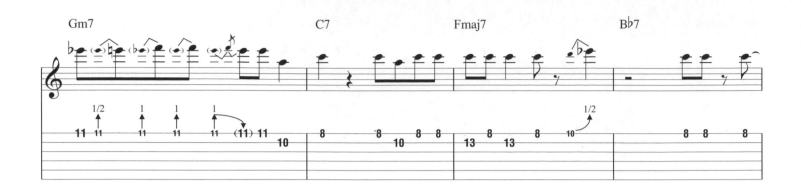

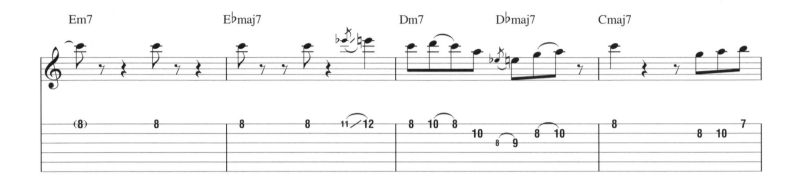

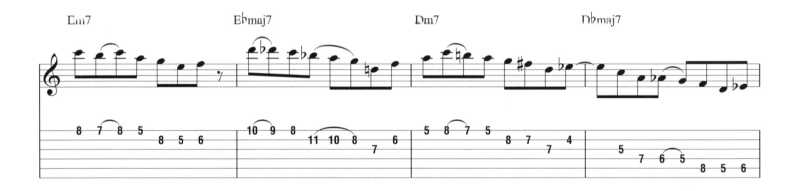

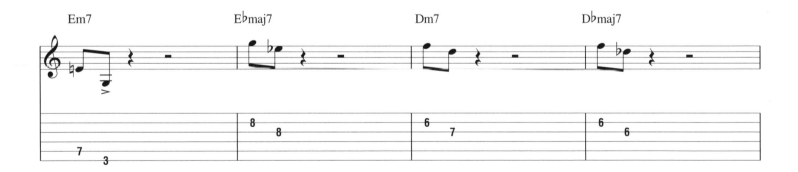

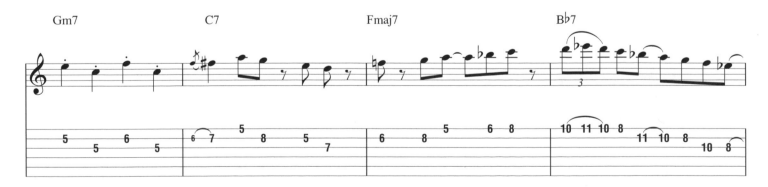

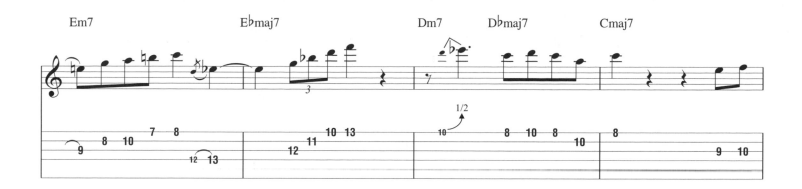

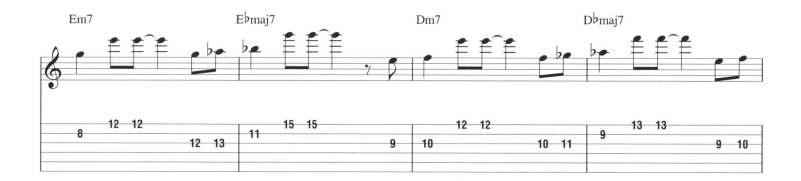

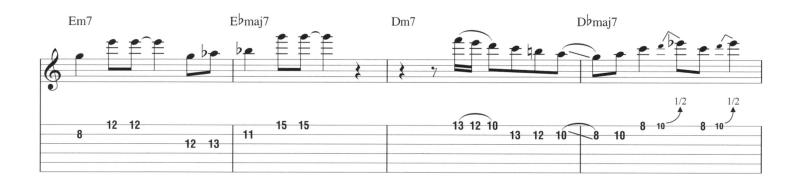

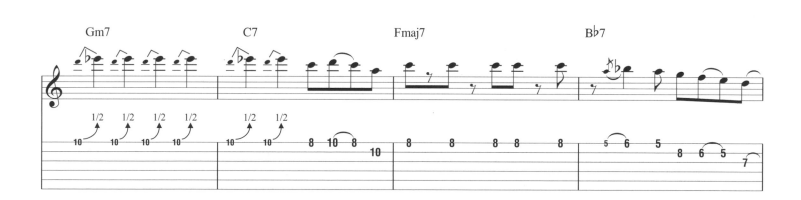

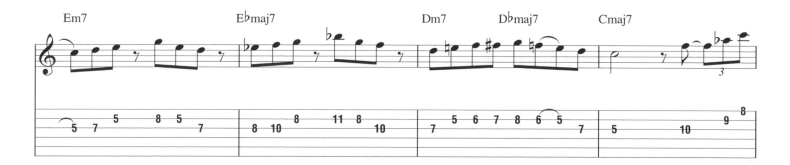

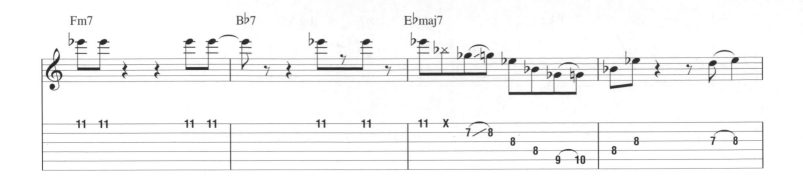

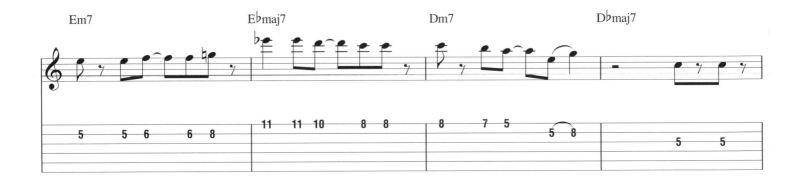

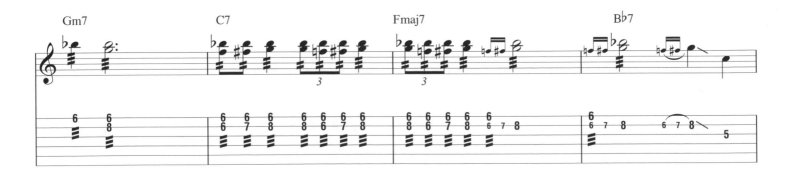

78

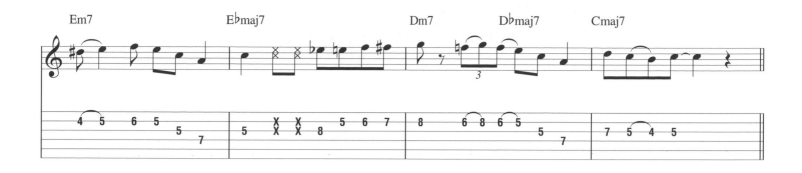

F

D.S. al Coda
(take repeat)

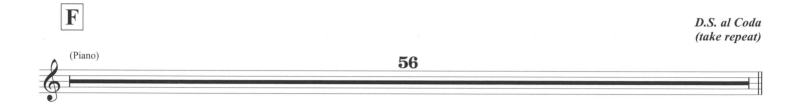

⊕ Coda

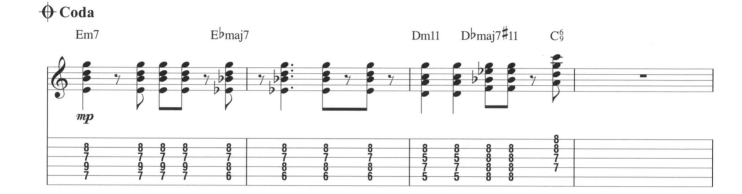

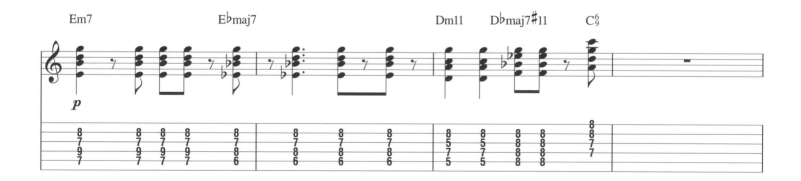

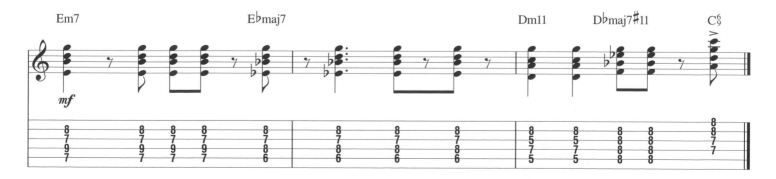

from *Thank You, Charlie Christian*

Pickly Wickly

By Herb Ellis

*Chord symbols reflect overall harmony.

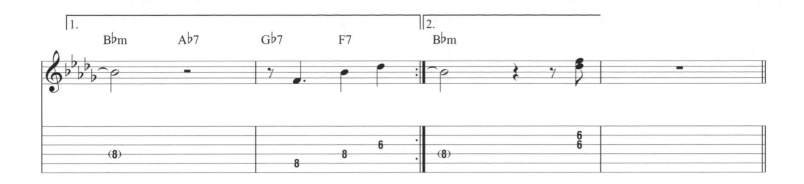

B

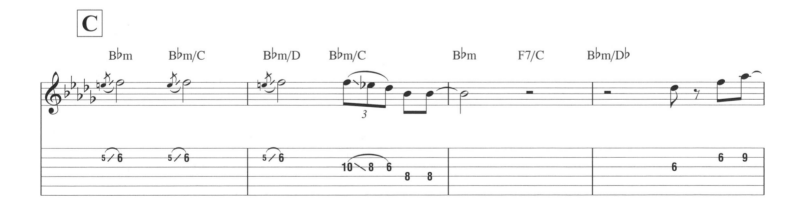

C

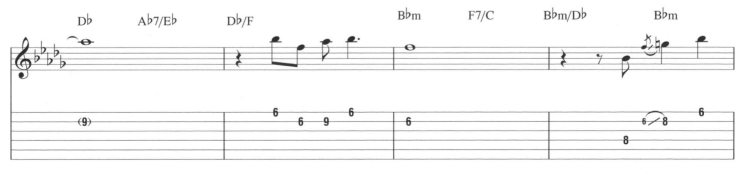

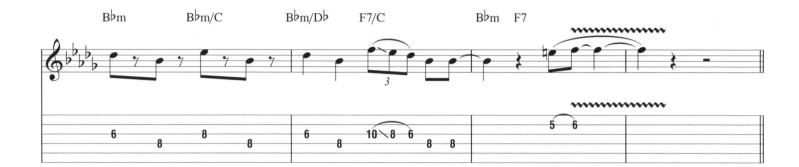

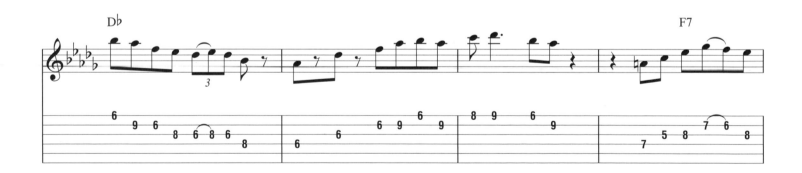

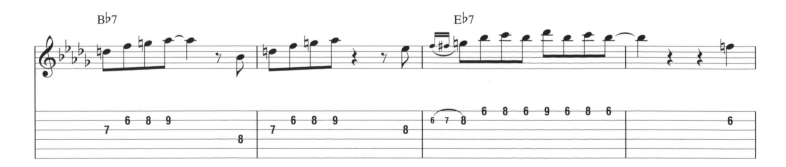

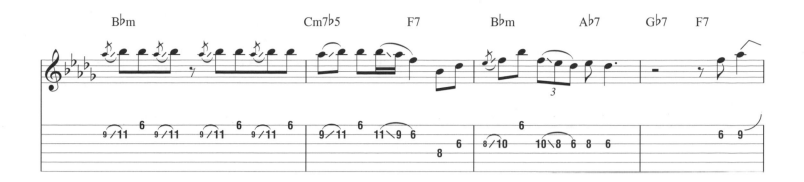

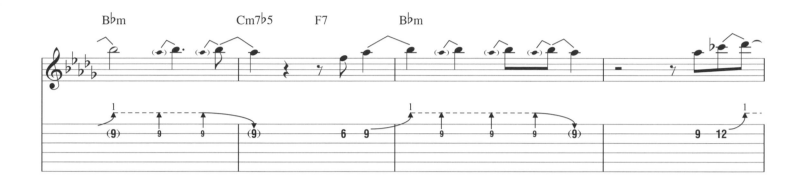

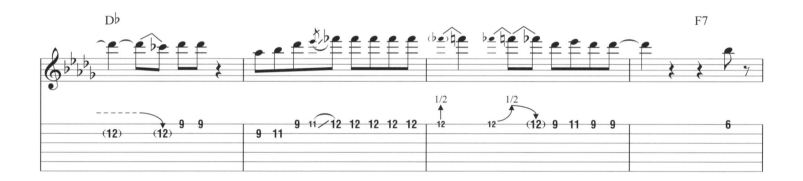

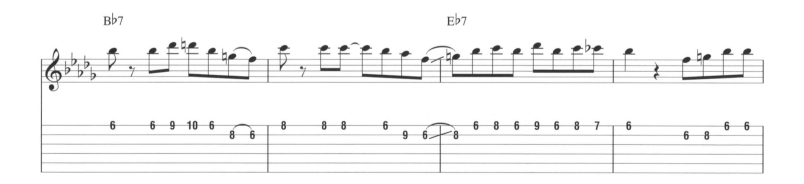

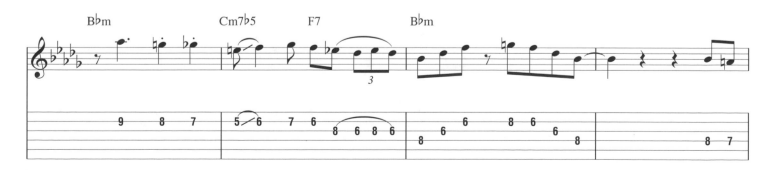

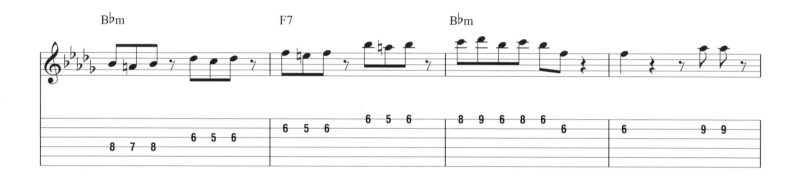

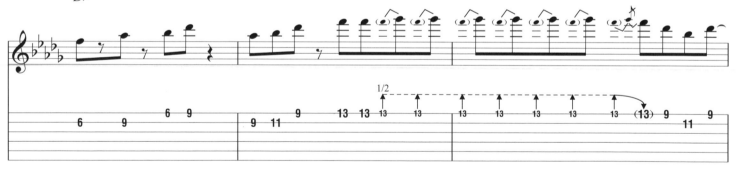

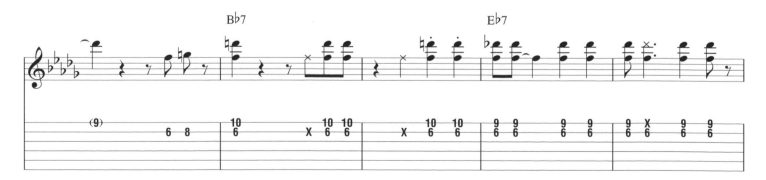

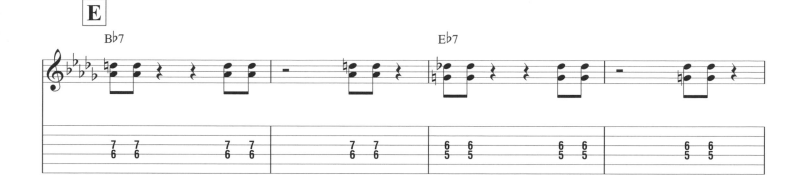

E

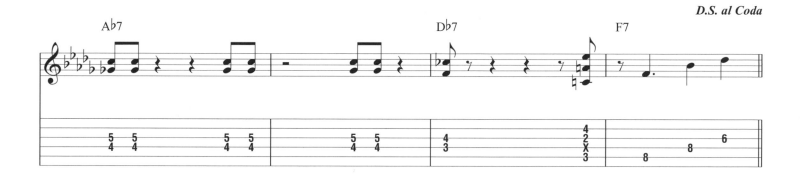

D.S. al Coda

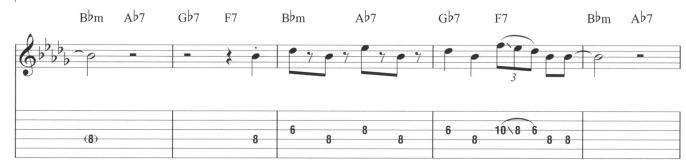

✛ **Coda**

from *Nothing but the Blues*

Royal Garden Blues

Words and Music by Clarence Williams and Spencer Williams

*Chord symbols reflect overall harmony.

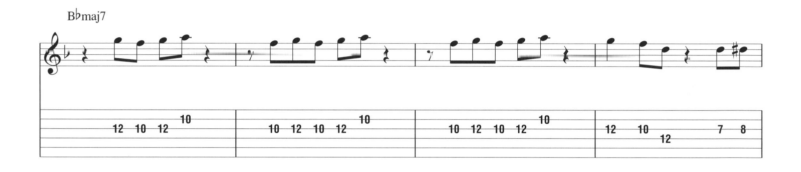

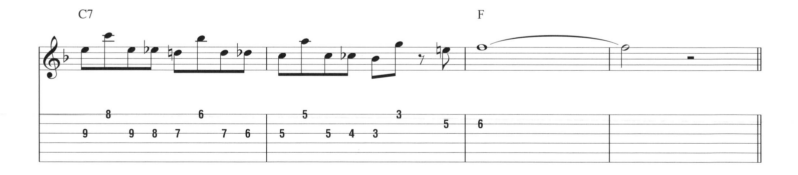

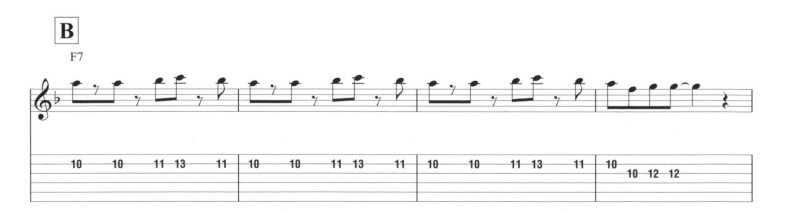

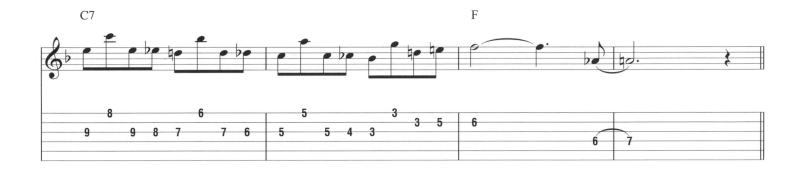

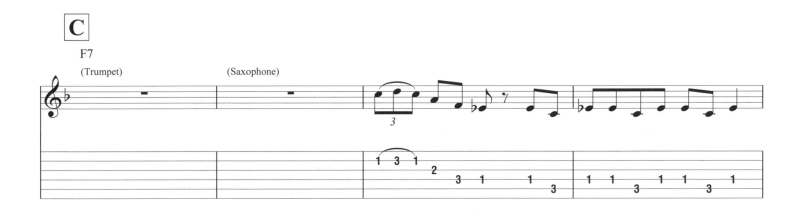

C

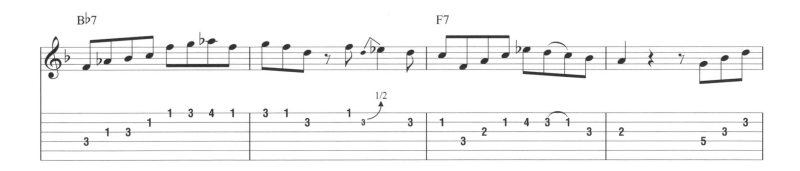

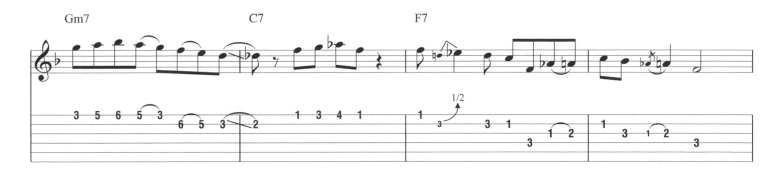

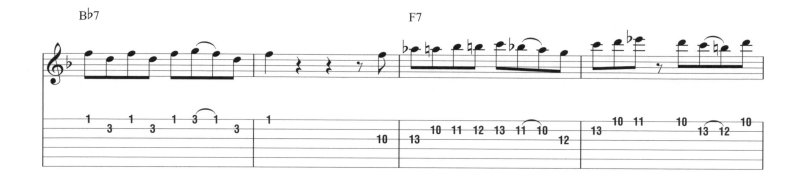

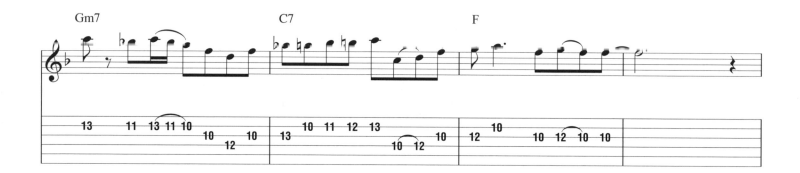

D

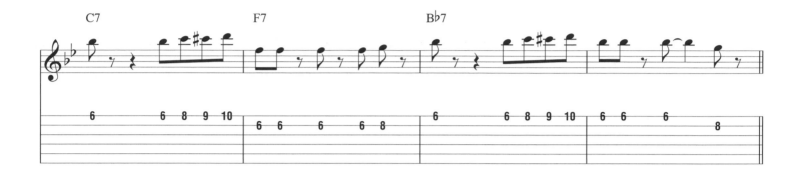

E

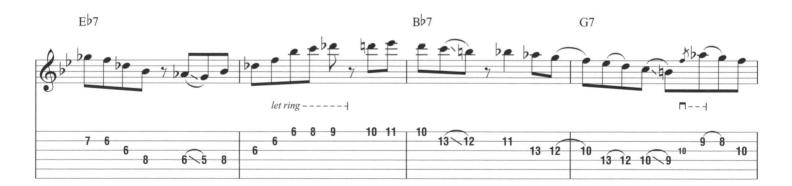

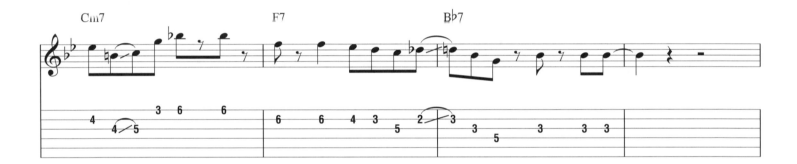

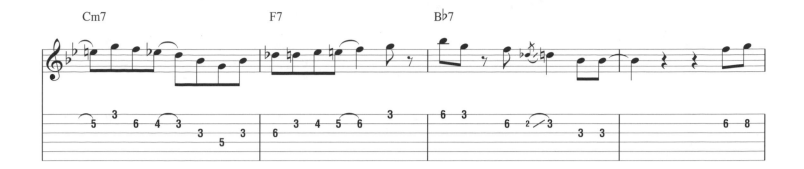

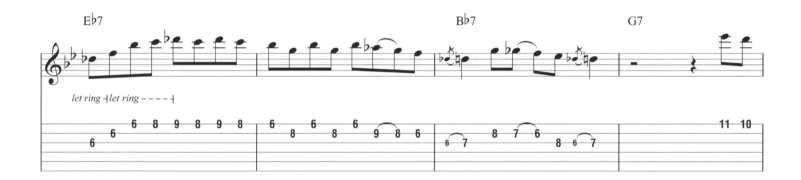

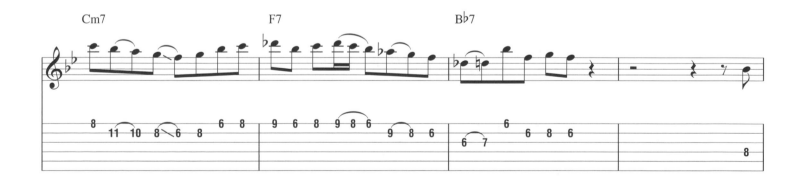

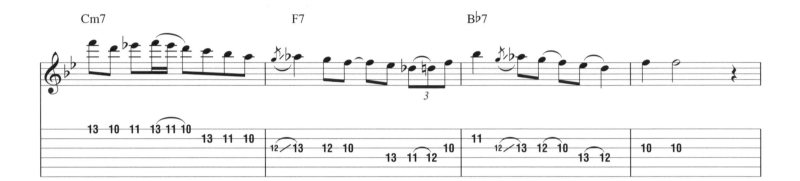

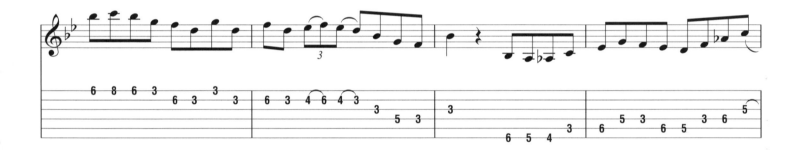

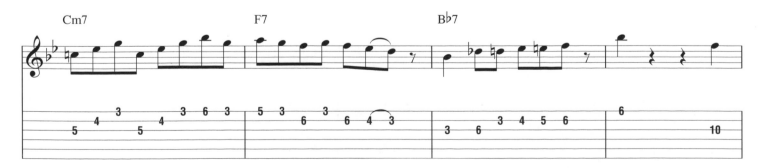

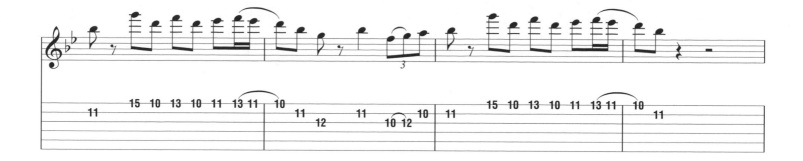

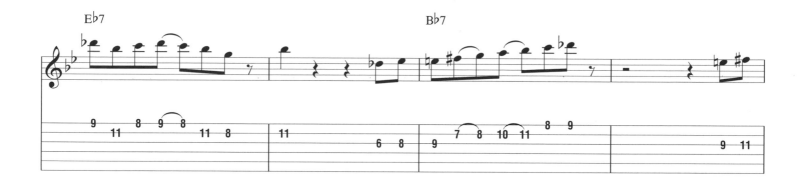

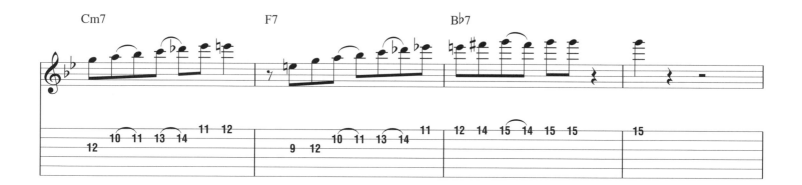

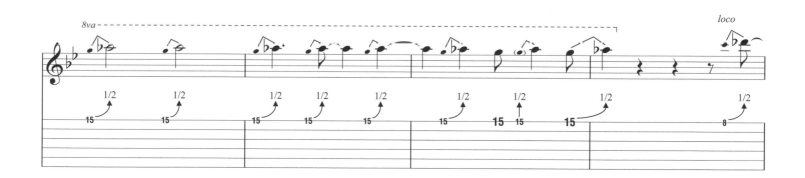

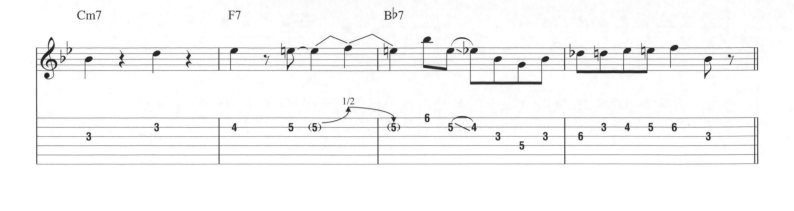

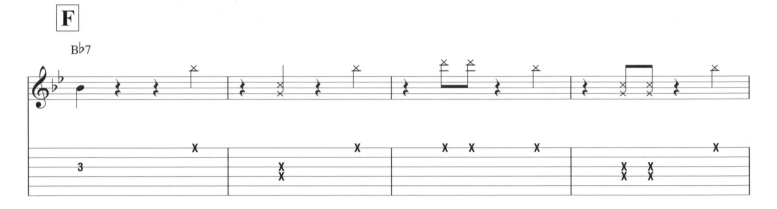

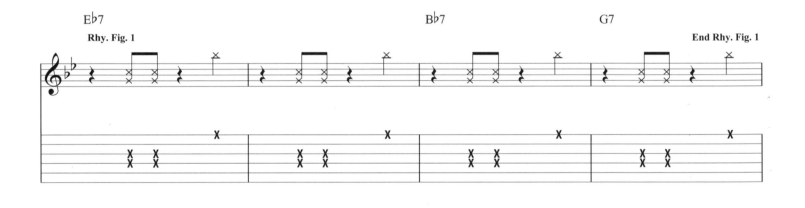

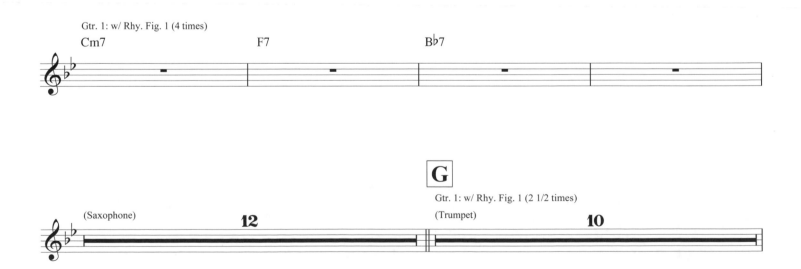

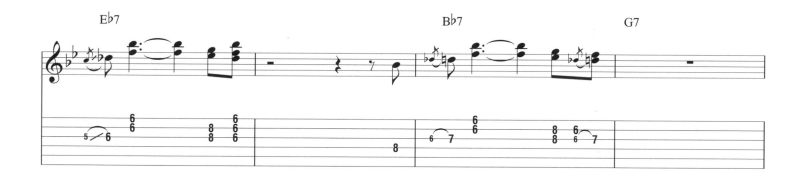

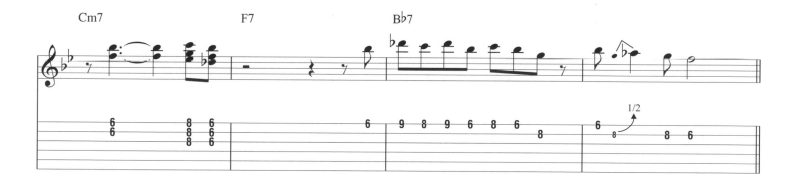

H

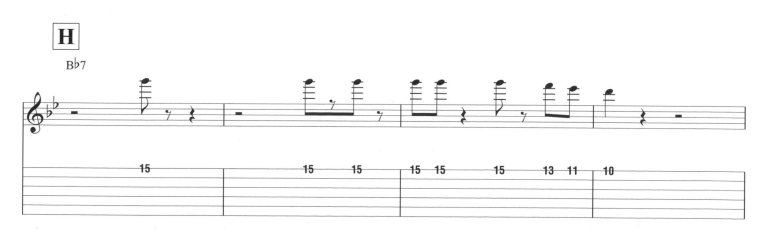

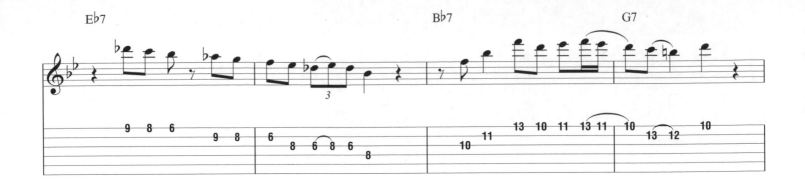

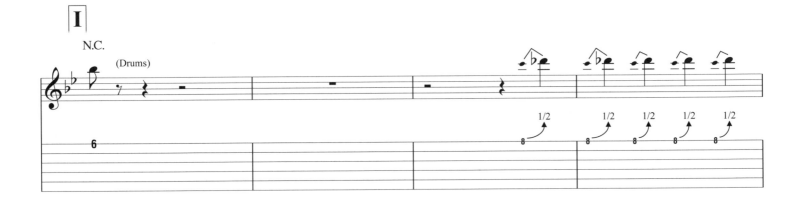

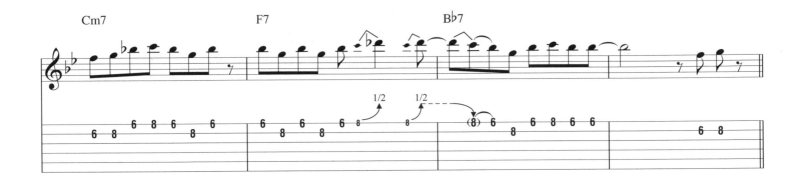

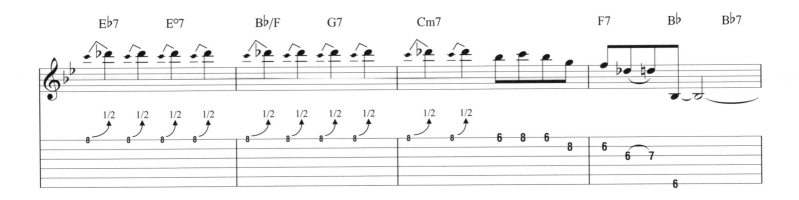

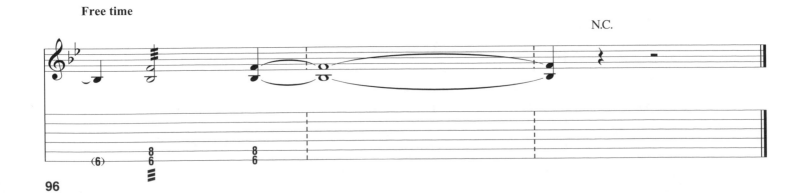

from *Ellis in Wonderland*

Somebody Loves Me

Music by George Gershwin
Lyrics by B.G. DeSylva and Ballard MacDonald
French Version by Emelia Renaud

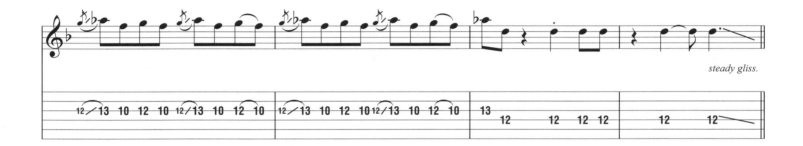

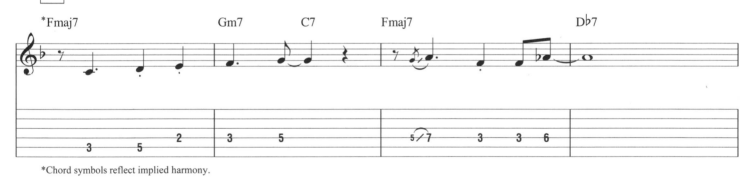

*Chord symbols reflect implied harmony.

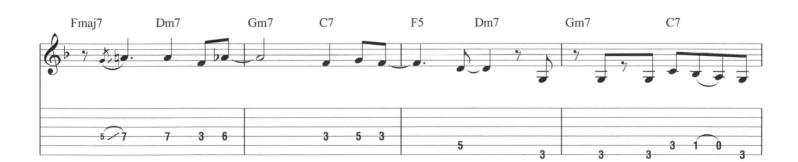

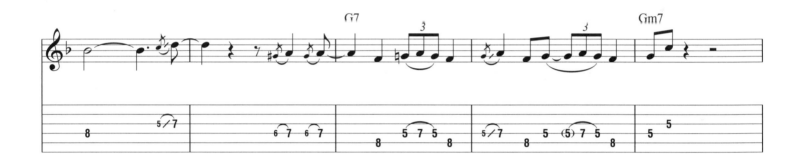

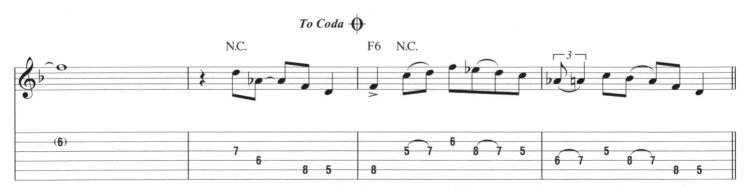

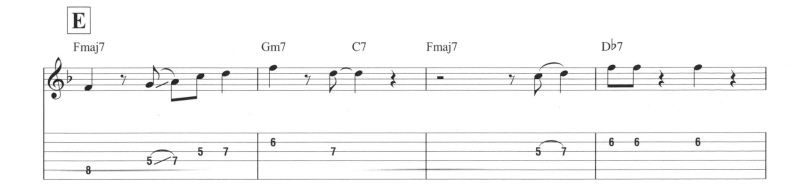

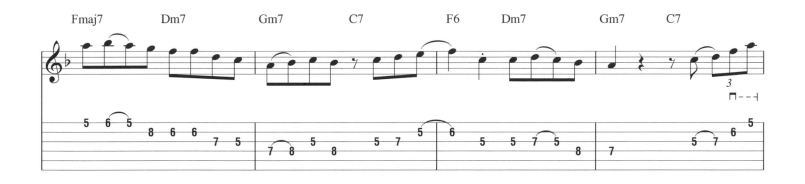

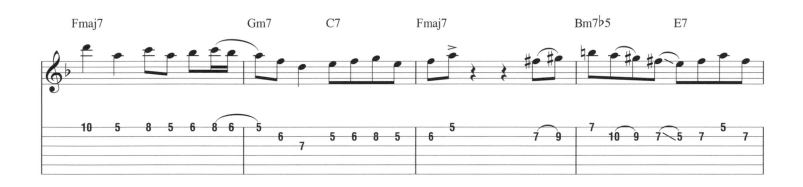

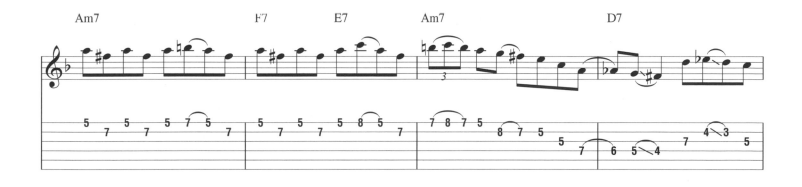

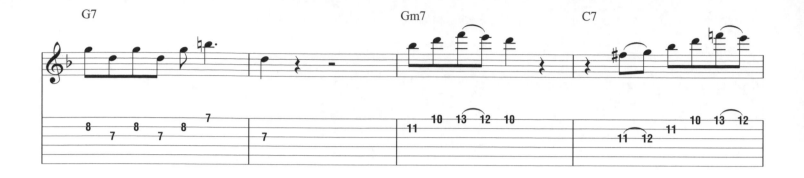

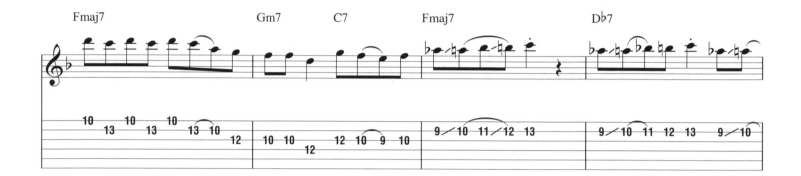

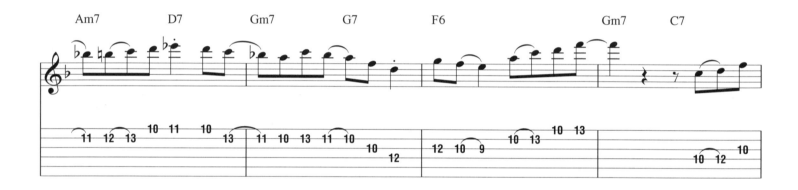

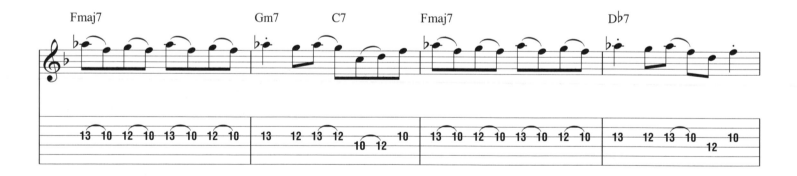

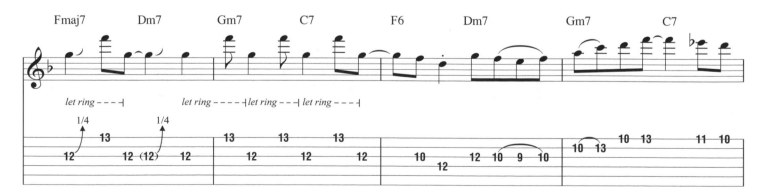

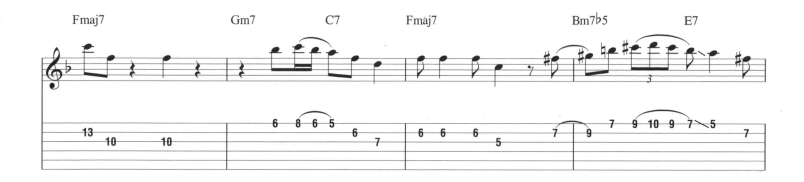

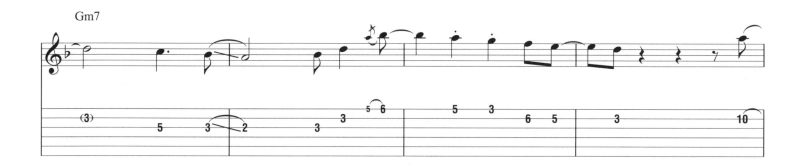

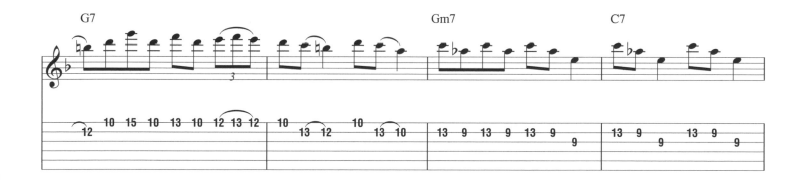

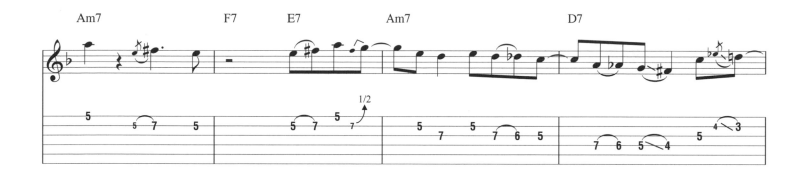

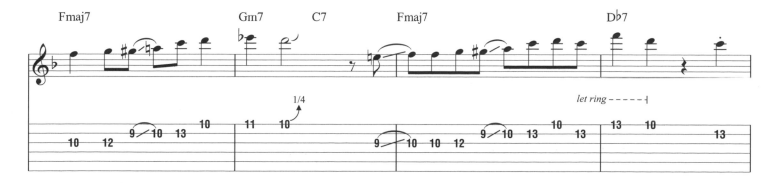

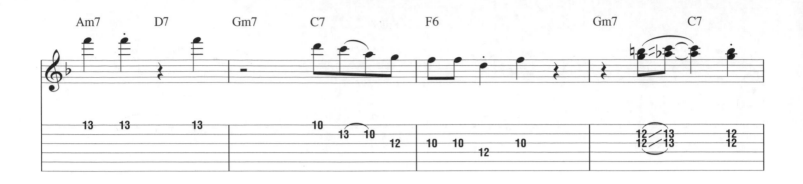

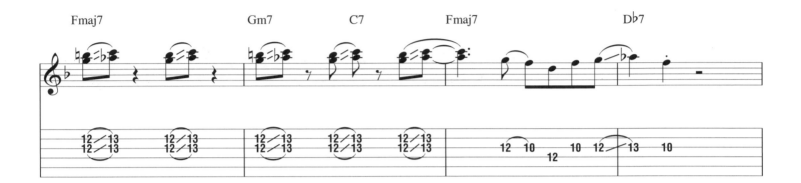

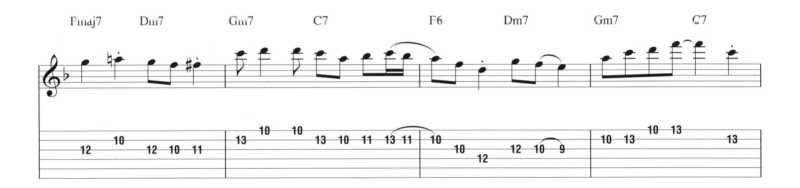

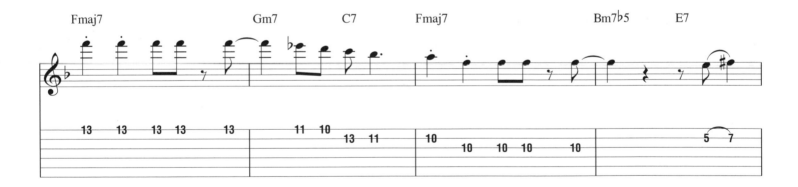

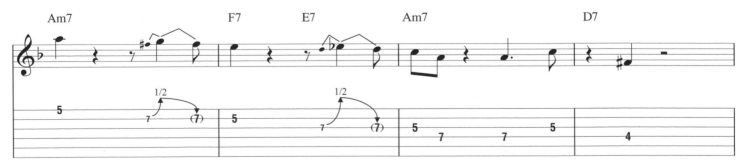

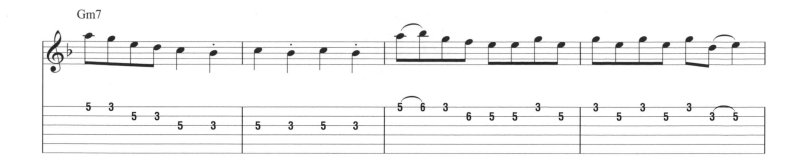

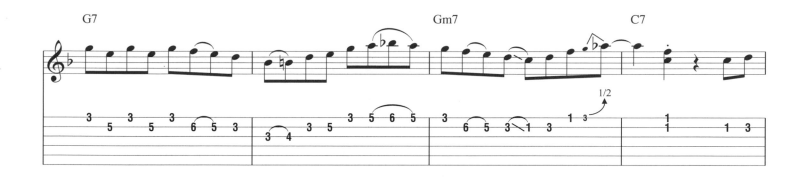

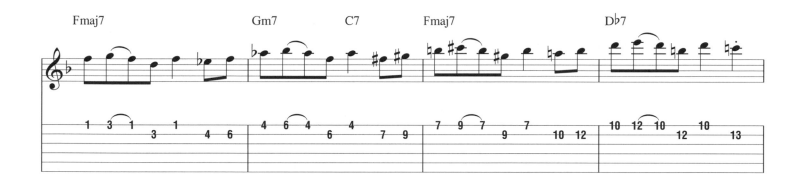

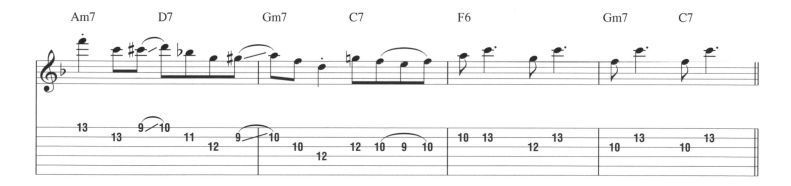

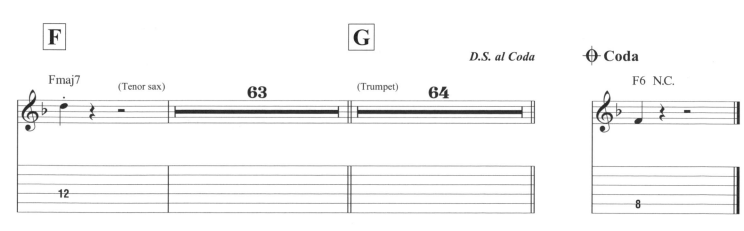

from *Arrival*
Stuffy
By Coleman Hawkins

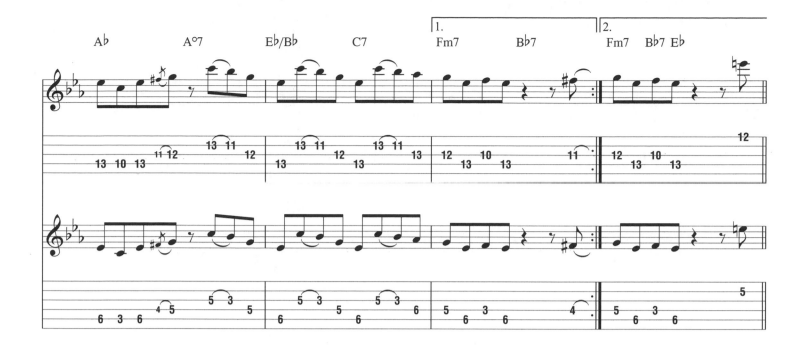

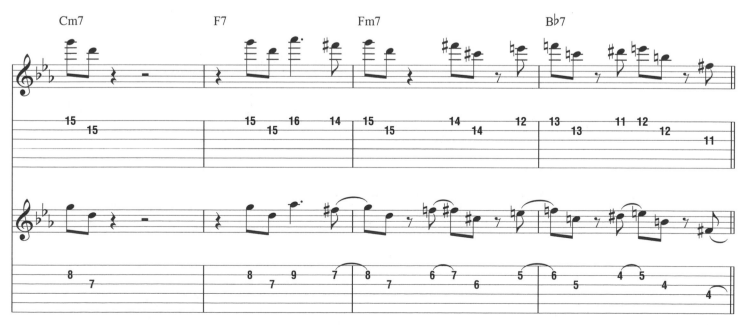

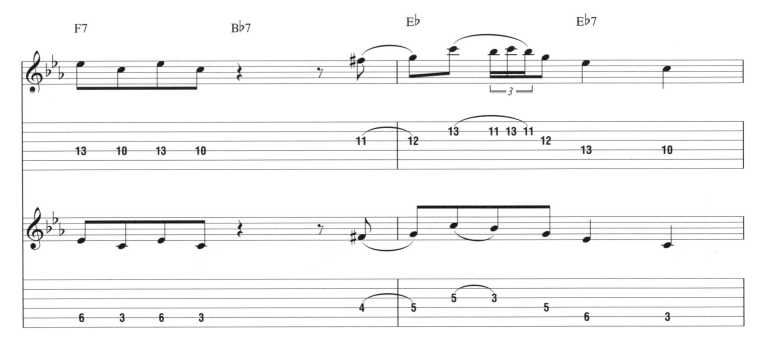

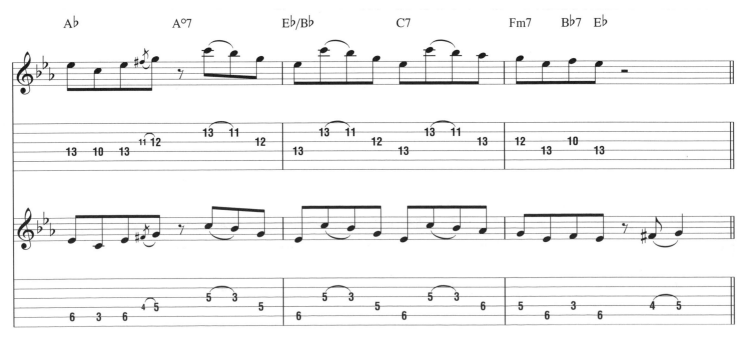

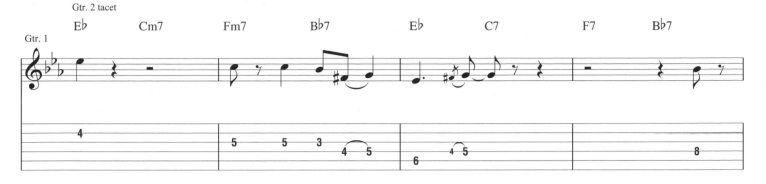

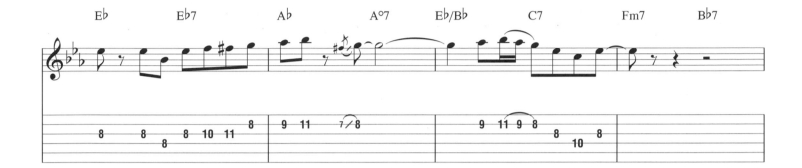

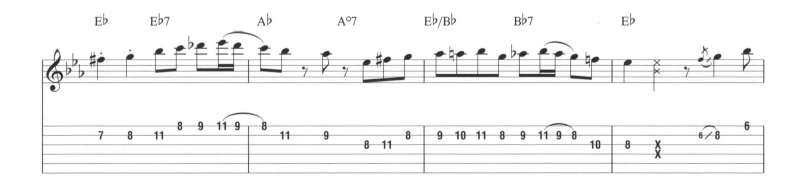

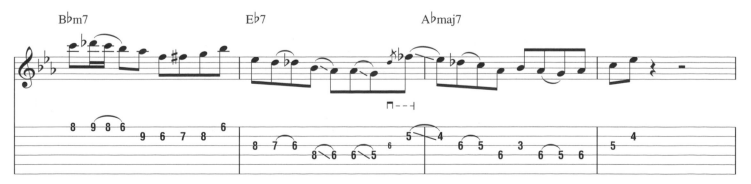

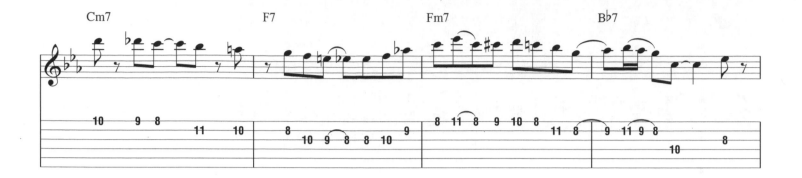

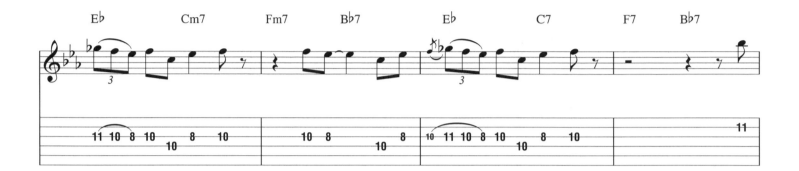

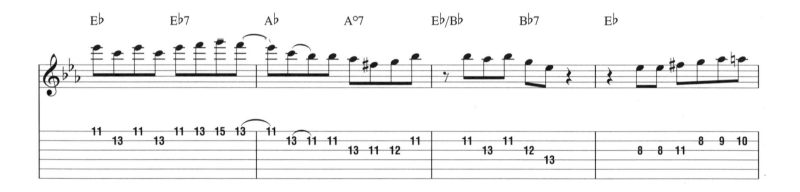

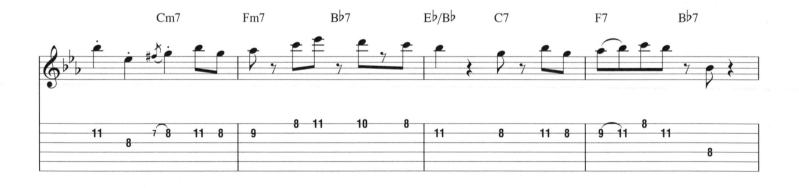

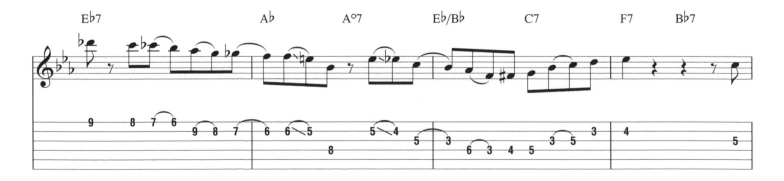

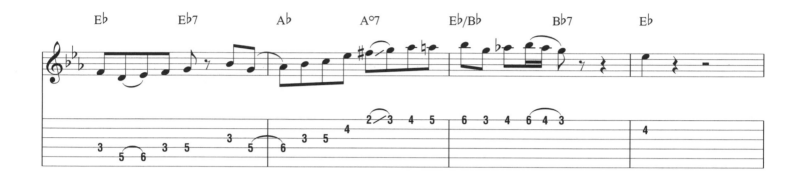

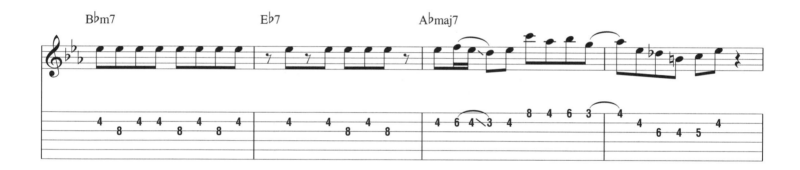

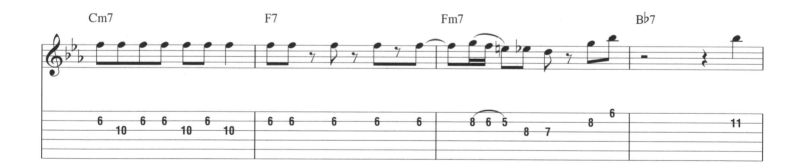

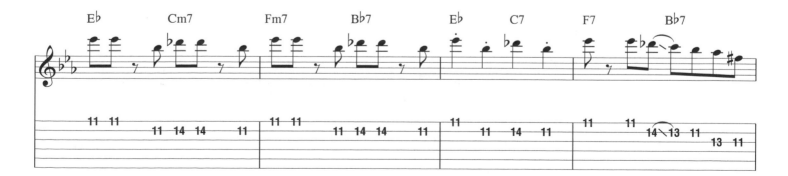

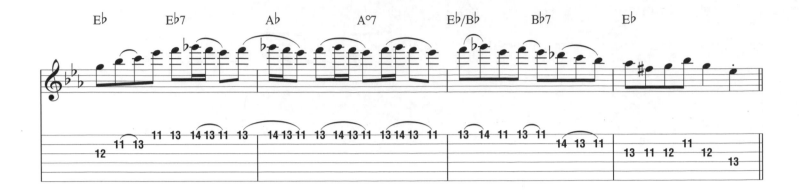

F

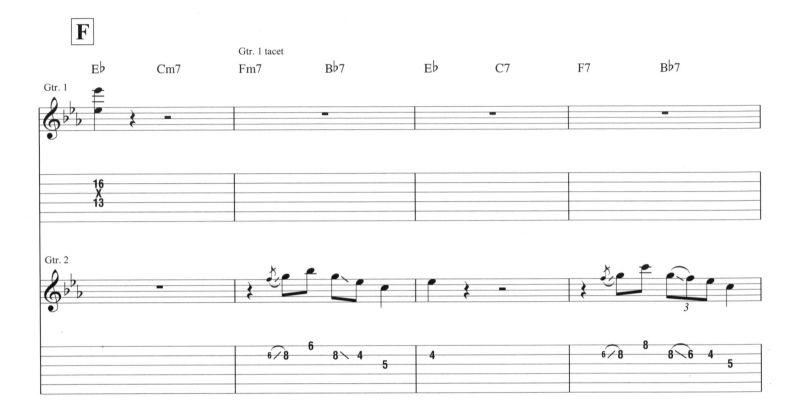

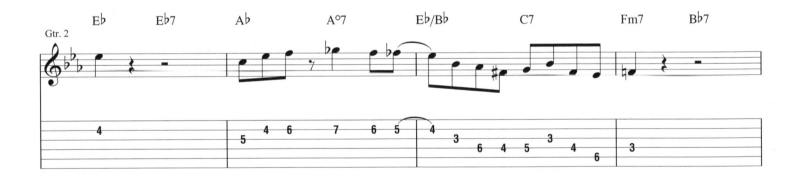

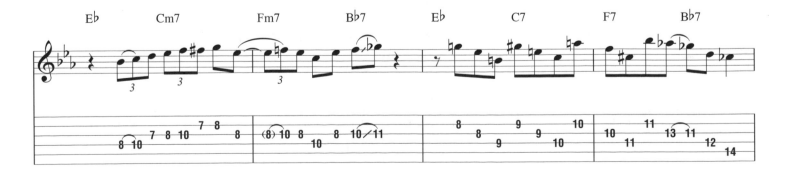

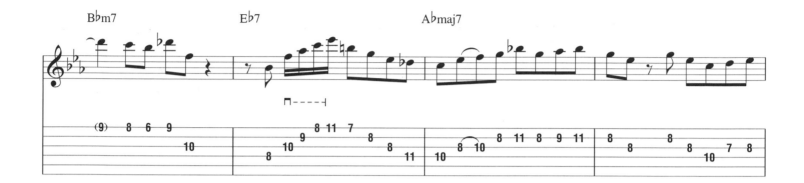

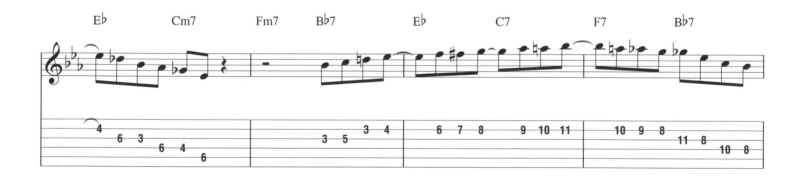

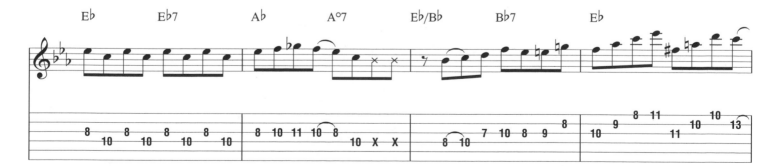

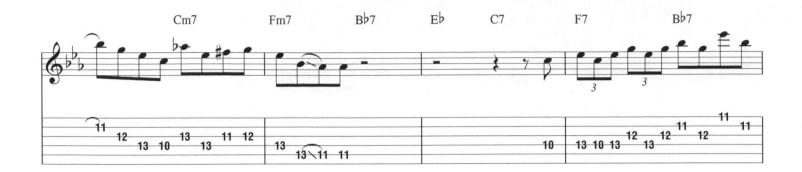

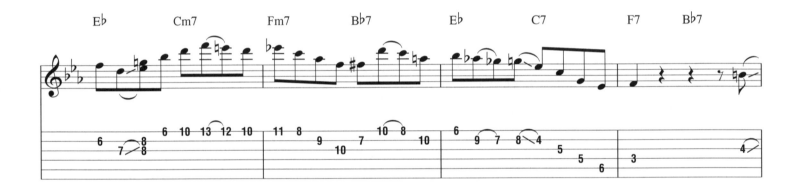

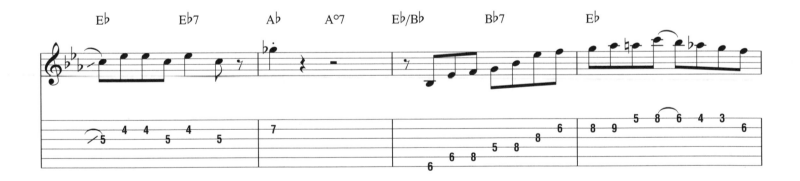

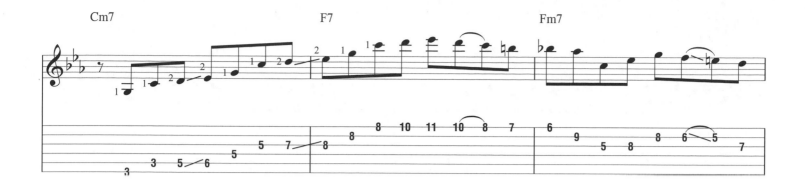

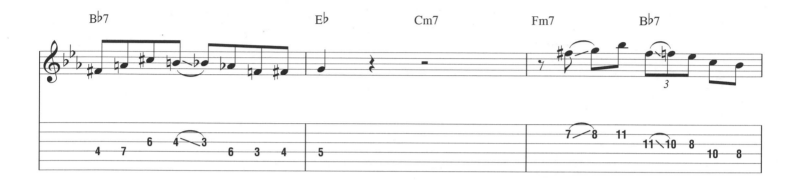

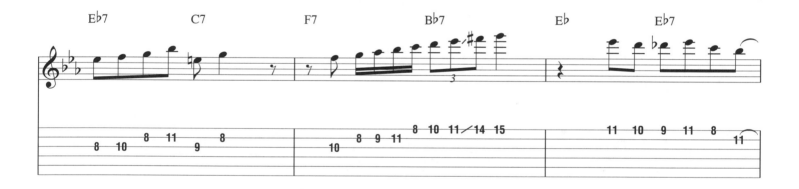

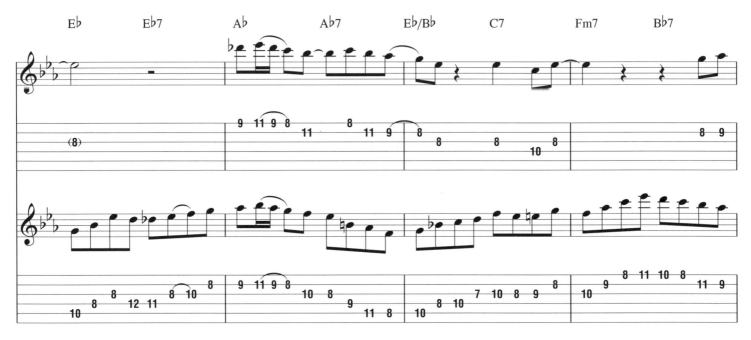

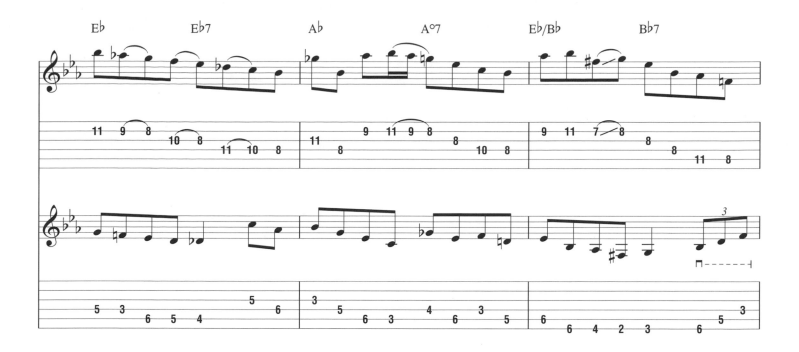

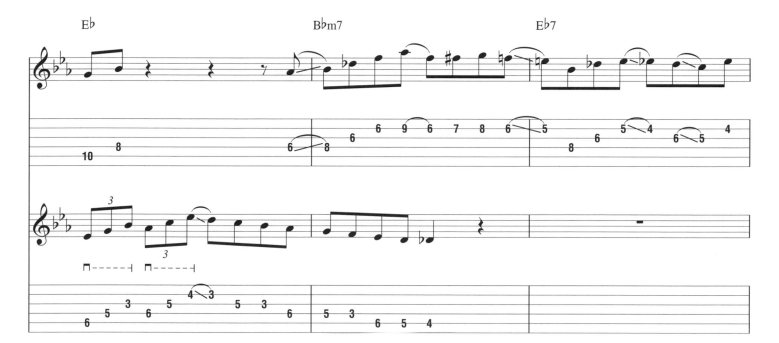

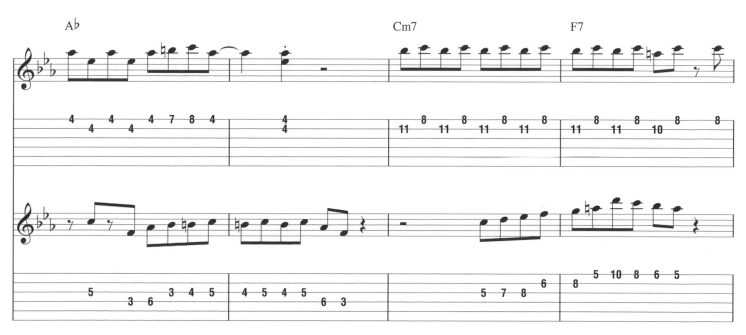

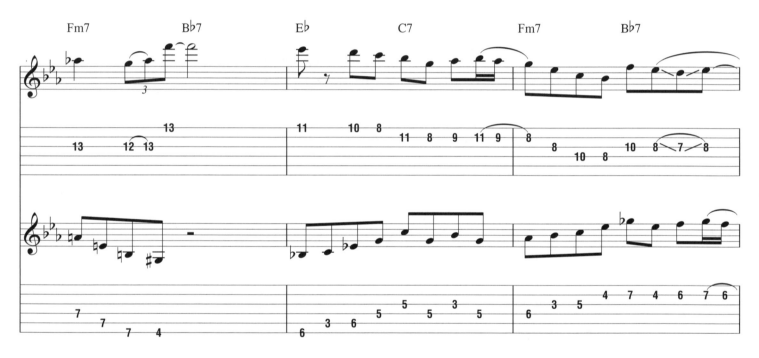

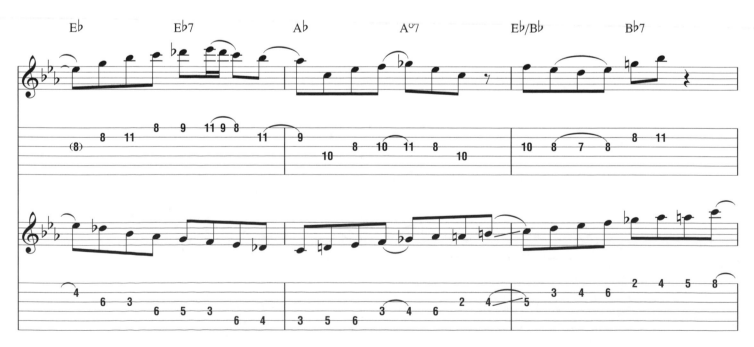

116

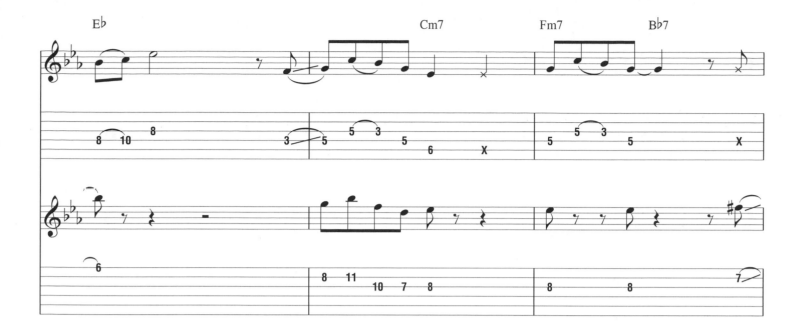

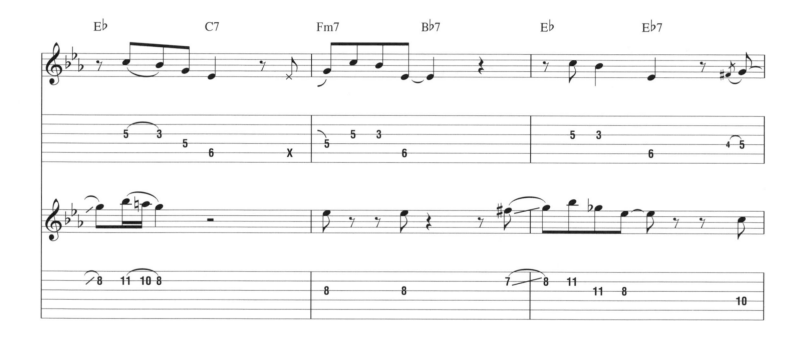

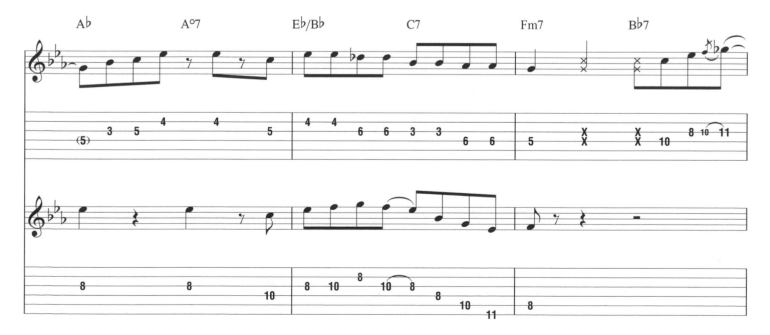

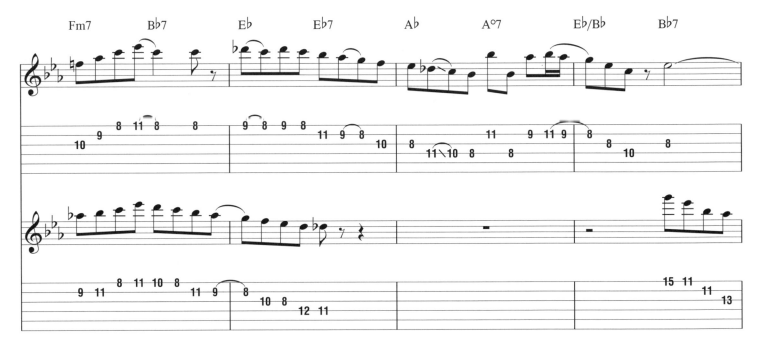

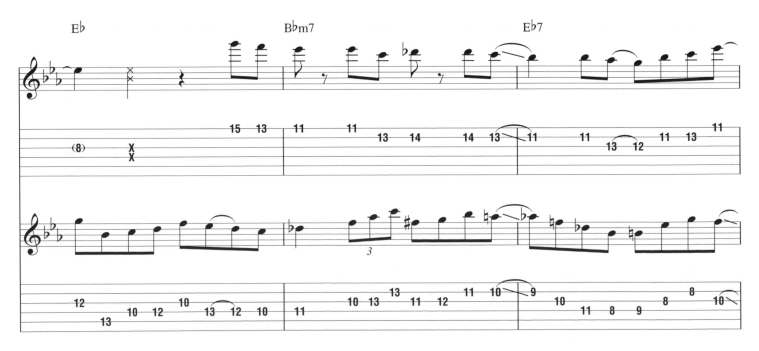

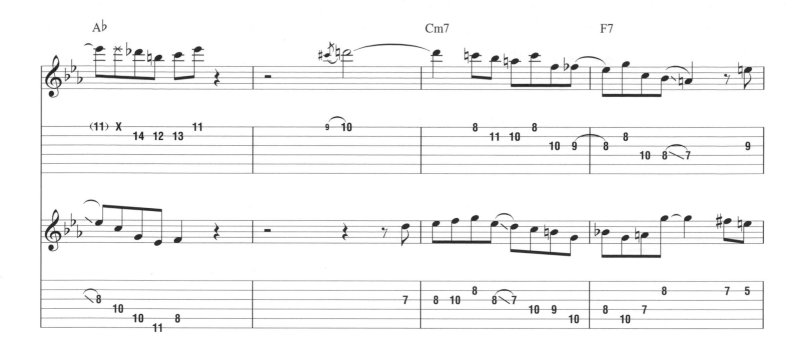

H

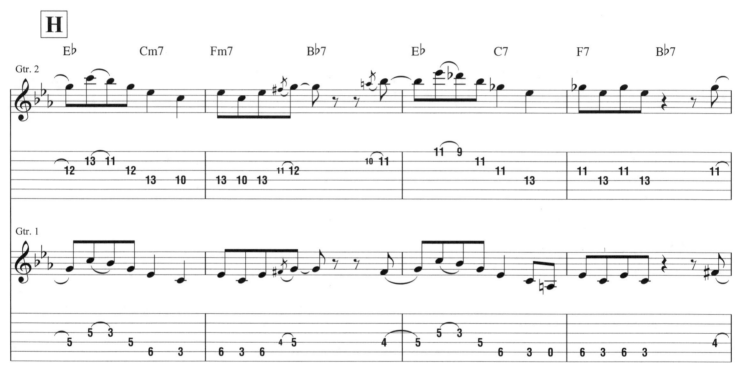

I

J

GUITAR NOTATION LEGEND

Guitar music can be notated three different ways: on a *musical staff*, in *tablature*, and in *rhythm slashes*.

RHYTHM SLASHES are written above the staff. Strum chords in the rhythm indicated. Use the chord diagrams found at the top of the first page of the transcription for the appropriate chord voicings. Round noteheads indicate single notes.

THE MUSICAL STAFF shows pitches and rhythms and is divided by bar lines into measures. Pitches are named after the first seven letters of the alphabet.

TABLATURE graphically represents the guitar fingerboard. Each horizontal line represents a string, and each number represents a fret.

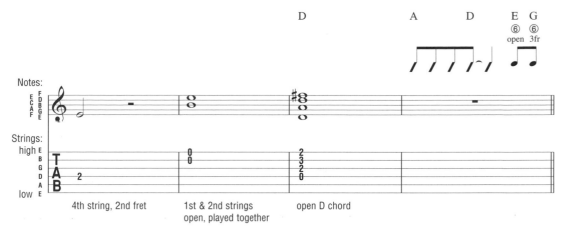

4th string, 2nd fret   1st & 2nd strings open, played together   open D chord

Definitions for Special Guitar Notation

HALF-STEP BEND: Strike the note and bend up 1/2 step.

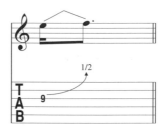

WHOLE-STEP BEND: Strike the note and bend up one step.

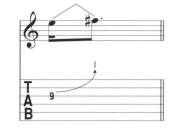

GRACE NOTE BEND: Strike the note and immediately bend up as indicated.

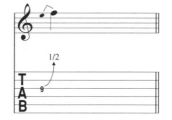

SLIGHT (MICROTONE) BEND: Strike the note and bend up 1/4 step.

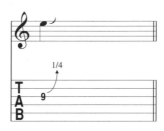

BEND AND RELEASE: Strike the note and bend up as indicated, then release back to the original note. Only the first note is struck.

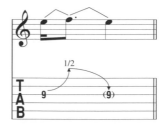

PRE-BEND: Bend the note as indicated, then strike it.

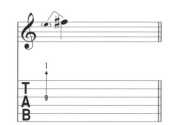

PRE-BEND AND RELEASE: Bend the note as indicated. Strike it and release the bend back to the original note.

UNISON BEND: Strike the two notes simultaneously and bend the lower note up to the pitch of the higher.

VIBRATO: The string is vibrated by rapidly bending and releasing the note with the fretting hand.

WIDE VIBRATO: The pitch is varied to a greater degree by vibrating with the fretting hand.

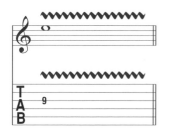

HAMMER-ON: Strike the first (lower) note with one finger, then sound the higher note (on the same string) with another finger by fretting it without picking.

PULL-OFF: Place both fingers on the notes to be sounded. Strike the first note and without picking, pull the finger off to sound the second (lower) note.

LEGATO SLIDE: Strike the first note and then slide the same fret-hand finger up or down to the second note. The second note is not struck.

SHIFT SLIDE: Same as legato slide, except the second note is struck.

TRILL: Very rapidly alternate between the notes indicated by continuously hammering on and pulling off.

TAPPING: Hammer ("tap") the fret indicated with the pick-hand index or middle finger and pull off to the note fretted by the fret hand.

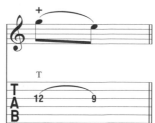

NATURAL HARMONIC: Strike the note while the fret-hand lightly touches the string directly over the fret indicated.

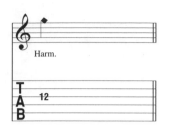

PINCH HARMONIC: The note is fretted normally and a harmonic is produced by adding the edge of the thumb or the tip of the index finger of the pick hand to the normal pick attack.

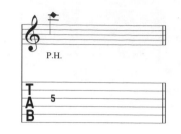

HARP HARMONIC: The note is fretted normally and a harmonic is produced by gently resting the pick hand's index finger directly above the indicated fret (in parentheses) while the pick hand's thumb or pick assists by plucking the appropriate string.

PICK SCRAPE: The edge of the pick is rubbed down (or up) the string, producing a scratchy sound.

MUFFLED STRINGS: A percussive sound is produced by laying the fret hand across the string(s) without depressing, and striking them with the pick hand.

PALM MUTING: The note is partially muted by the pick hand lightly touching the string(s) just before the bridge.

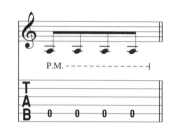

RAKE: Drag the pick across the strings indicated with a single motion.

TREMOLO PICKING: The note is picked as rapidly and continuously as possible.

ARPEGGIATE: Play the notes of the chord indicated by quickly rolling them from bottom to top.

VIBRATO BAR DIVE AND RETURN: The pitch of the note or chord is dropped a specified number of steps (in rhythm), then returned to the original pitch.

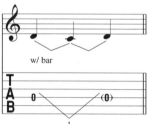

VIBRATO BAR SCOOP: Depress the bar just before striking the note, then quickly release the bar.

VIBRATO BAR DIP: Strike the note and then immediately drop a specified number of steps, then release back to the original pitch.

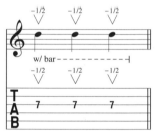

Additional Musical Definitions

(accent)	• Accentuate note (play it louder).	**Rhy. Fig.**	• Label used to recall a recurring accompaniment pattern (usually chordal).
(accent)	• Accentuate note with great intensity.	**Riff**	• Label used to recall composed, melodic lines (usually single notes) which recur.
(staccato)	• Play the note short.	**Fill**	• Label used to identify a brief melodic figure which is to be inserted into the arrangement.
⊓	• Downstroke	**Rhy. Fill**	• A chordal version of a Fill.
V	• Upstroke	tacet	• Instrument is silent (drops out).
D.S. al Coda	• Go back to the sign (𝄋), then play until the measure marked "*To Coda*," then skip to the section labelled "**Coda**."		• Repeat measures between signs.
D.C. al Fine	• Go back to the beginning of the song and play until the measure marked "*Fine*" (end).		• When a repeated section has different endings, play the first ending only the first time and the second ending only the second time.

NOTE: Tablature numbers in parentheses mean:
    1. The note is being sustained over a system (note in standard notation is tied), or
    2. The note is sustained, but a new articulation (such as a hammer-on, pull-off, slide or vibrato) begins, or
    3. The note is a barely audible "ghost" note (note in standard notation is also in parentheses).

ARTIST TRANSCRIPTIONS

Artist Transcriptions are authentic, note-for-note transcriptions of today's hottest artists in jazz, pop and rock. These outstanding, accurate arrangements are In an easy-to-read format which includes all essential lines. **Artist Transcriptions** can be used to perform, sequence or for reference.

JAZZ GUITAR CHORD MELODY SOLOS

This series features chord melody arrangements in standard notation and tablature of songs for intermediate guitarists.

ALL-TIME STANDARDS *INCLUDES TAB*

27 songs, including: All of Me • Bewitched • Come Fly with Me • A Fine Romance • Georgia on My Mind • How High the Moon • I'll Never Smile Again • I've Got You Under My Skin • It's De-Lovely • It's Only a Paper Moon • My Romance • Satin Doll • The Surrey with the Fringe on Top • Yesterdays • and more.

00699757 Solo Guitar $14.99

CHRISTMAS CAROLS *INCLUDES TAB*

26 songs, including: Auld Lang Syne • Away in a Manger • Deck the Hall • God Rest Ye Merry, Gentlemen • Good King Wenceslas • Here We Come A-Wassailing • It Came upon the Midnight Clear • Joy to the World • O Holy Night • O Little Town of Bethlehem • Silent Night • Toyland • We Three Kings of Orient Are • and more.

00701697 Solo Guitar $12.99

DISNEY SONGS *INCLUDES TAB*

27 songs, including: Beauty and the Beast • Can You Feel the Love Tonight • Candle on the Water • Colors of the Wind • A Dream Is a Wish Your Heart Makes • Heigh-Ho • Some Day My Prince Will Come • Under the Sea • When You Wish upon a Star • A Whole New World (Aladdin's Theme) • Zip-A-Dee-Doo-Dah • and more.

00701902 Solo Guitar $14.99

DUKE ELLINGTON *INCLUDES TAB*

25 songs, including: C-Jam Blues • Caravan • Do Nothin' Till You Hear from Me • Don't Get Around Much Anymore • I Got It Bad and That Ain't Good • I'm Just a Lucky So and So • In a Sentimental Mood • It Don't Mean a Thing (If It Ain't Got That Swing) • Mood Indigo • Perdido • Prelude to a Kiss • Satin Doll • and more.

00700636 Solo Guitar $12.99

FAVORITE STANDARDS *INCLUDES TAB*

27 songs, including: All the Way • Autumn in New York • Blue Skies • Cheek to Cheek • Don't Get Around Much Anymore • How Deep Is the Ocean • I'll Be Seeing You • Isn't It Romantic? • It Could Happen to You • The Lady Is a Tramp • Moon River • Speak Low • Take the "A" Train • Willow Weep for Me • Witchcraft • and more.

00699756 Solo Guitar $14.99

FINGERPICKING JAZZ STANDARDS *INCLUDES TAB*

15 songs: Autumn in New York • Body and Soul • Can't Help Lovin' Dat Man • Easy Living • A Fine Romance • Have You Met Miss Jones? • I'm Beginning to See the Light • It Could Happen to You • My Romance • Stella by Starlight • Tangerine • The Very Thought of You • The Way You Look Tonight • When Sunny Gets Blue • Yesterdays.

00699840 Solo Guitar $7.99

JAZZ BALLADS *INCLUDES TAB*

27 songs, including: Body and Soul • Darn That Dream • Easy to Love (You'd Be So Easy to Love) • Here's That Rainy Day • In a Sentimental Mood • Misty • My Foolish Heart • My Funny Valentine • The Nearness of You • Stella by Starlight • Time After Time • The Way You Look Tonight • When Sunny Gets Blue • and more.

00699755 Solo Guitar $14.99

JAZZ CLASSICS *INCLUDES TAB*

27 songs, including: Blue in Green • Bluesette • Bouncing with Bud • Cast Your Fate to the Wind • Con Alma • Doxy • Epistrophy • Footprints • Giant Steps • Invitation • Lullaby of Birdland • Lush Life • A Night in Tunisia • Nuages • Ruby, My Dear • St. Thomas • Stolen Moments • Waltz for Debby • Yardbird Suite • and more.

00699758 Solo Guitar $14.99

Prices, content, and availability subject to change without notice. | Disney characters and artwork ©Disney Enterprises, Inc.

> " Well-crafted arrangements that sound great and are still accessible to most players. "
> – *Guitar Edge* magazine

HAL•LEONARD®

www.halleonard.com